First World War
and Army of Occupation
War Diary
France, Belgium and Germany

2 INDIAN CAVALRY DIVISION
Secunderabad Cavalry Brigade
'N' Battery Royal Horse Artillery,
Brigade Signal Troop,
Brigade Machine Gun Squadron
and Mobile Veterinary Section
12 March 1914 - 31 December 1916

WO95/1188

The Naval & Military Press Ltd
www.nmarchive.com
Published in association with The National Archives

Published by

The Naval & Military Press Ltd

Unit 10 Ridgewood Industrial Park,

Uckfield, East Sussex,

TN22 5QE England

Tel: +44 (0) 1825 749494

www.naval-military-press.com

www.nmarchive.com

This diary has been reprinted in facsimile from the original. Any imperfections are inevitably reproduced and the quality may fall short of modern type and cartographic standards.

© **Crown Copyright**
Images reproduced by permission of The National Archives, London, England, 2015.

Contents

Document type	Place/Title	Date From	Date To
Miscellaneous	B.E.F. France & Flanders. 2 Indian Cav Division Secunderabad Cav Brigade 'N' Bty Royal Horse Artillery.		
Miscellaneous	B.E.F. France & Flanders. 2 Indian Cav Division.		
Miscellaneous	2 Ind Cav Div Secunderabad Bde "N" Bty R.H.A 1914 Aug-1916 Dec		
Miscellaneous	War Diary Of 'N' Battery R.H.A. From 9.8.14. To 31.12.14 Volume 1 Pp To		
War Diary	Trimulgherry	09/08/1914	15/08/1914
War Diary	Bolarum	26/08/1914	26/08/1914
War Diary	Trimulgherry	30/08/1914	30/08/1914
War Diary	Bombay	01/09/1914	03/09/1914
War Diary	Aden	11/09/1914	11/09/1914
War Diary	Redsea	12/09/1914	14/09/1914
War Diary	Suez	17/09/1914	17/09/1914
War Diary	Port Said	18/09/1914	18/09/1914
War Diary	Nr Lwant	19/09/1914	19/09/1914
War Diary	Oh Malta	22/09/1914	22/09/1914
War Diary	Marseilles	26/09/1914	05/10/1914
War Diary	Orleans	07/10/1914	30/10/1914
War Diary	Berguette	01/11/1914	02/11/1914
War Diary	Pont De Hem	05/11/1914	12/11/1914
War Diary	In Essars	13/11/1914	13/11/1914
War Diary	Pont De Hem	14/11/1914	15/11/1914
War Diary	Pont Tournant	16/11/1914	16/11/1914
War Diary	Richebourg	17/11/1914	30/11/1914
War Diary	Hinges	01/12/1914	01/12/1914
War Diary	Avelette	02/12/1914	19/12/1914
War Diary	Le Touret	20/12/1914	26/12/1914
War Diary	La Roupie	27/12/1914	31/12/1914
Heading	War Diary Of "N" Battery R.H.A. From 1st January 1915 To. 31st January 1915		
War Diary	La Roupie	01/01/1915	31/01/1915
Heading	War Diary Of "N" Battery R.H.A. From 1st February 1915 To 28th February 1915.		
War Diary	La Roupie	01/02/1915	28/02/1915
War Diary		11/02/1915	11/02/1915
War Diary		08/02/1915	08/02/1915
Heading	War Diary Of "N" Battery R.H.A. From 1st March 1915 To. 31st March 1915		
War Diary	La Roupie	01/03/1915	03/03/1915
War Diary	Pont Du Hem	04/03/1915	12/03/1915
War Diary	Neuve Chapelle	12/03/1914	12/03/1914
War Diary	Pont Du Hem	13/03/1914	16/03/1914
War Diary	2 Miles E Of Laventie	17/03/1915	31/03/1915
Heading	War Diary Of "N" Battery R.H.A. From 1st April 1915 To, 30th April 1915		
War Diary	2 Miles E Of Laventie	01/04/1915	02/04/1915
War Diary	Nielles	03/04/1915	06/04/1915
War Diary	Rebecq	07/04/1915	25/04/1915

War Diary	L'Hey	26/04/1915	28/04/1915
War Diary	Proven	29/04/1915	30/04/1915
Heading	War Diary Of 'N' Battery R.H.A. From 1st Mary 1915 To 31st May 1915		
War Diary	Proven	01/05/1915	04/05/1915
War Diary	Richebourg St Vaast	05/05/1915	24/05/1915
War Diary	Dennebroeuck	25/05/1915	01/06/1915
Heading	War Diary Of 'N' Battery R.H.A. From 1st June 1915 To 30th June 1915		
War Diary		01/06/1915	30/06/1915
Heading	War Diary of 'N' Battery R.H.A. From 1st July 1915 To 31st July 1915		
War Diary	Dennebroeuck	01/07/1915	31/07/1915
War Diary		10/07/1915	30/07/1915
Heading	War Diary Of "N" Battery R.H.A. From 1st August 1915 To 31st August 1915		
War Diary		01/08/1915	03/08/1915
War Diary	Inclusive	04/08/1915	31/08/1915
Miscellaneous	War Diary Of 'N' Battery R.H.A. From 1st September 1915 To 30th September 1915		
War Diary	In Action	01/09/1915	01/09/1915
War Diary	Near Mesnil	02/09/1915	15/09/1915
War Diary	Le Mesge	16/09/1915	30/09/1915
Heading	War Diary Of 'N' Battery R.H.A. From 1st October 1915 To 31 October 1915		
War Diary	Gorges	01/10/1915	10/10/1915
War Diary	Fraqueville	11/10/1915	13/10/1915
War Diary	Bussus	13/10/1915	24/10/1915
War Diary	St Maxent	24/10/1915	31/10/1915
War Diary	En Vimeux	31/10/1915	31/10/1915
Heading	War Diary Of "N" Battery Royal Horse Artillery From 1st November 1915 To 30th November 1915		
War Diary	St Maxent En Vimeu	01/11/1915	18/11/1915
Heading	War Diary Of 'N' Battery Royal Horse Artillery From 1st December 1915 To 31st December 1915		
War Diary	St Maxent En Vimeu	01/12/1915	31/12/1915
Heading	War Diary Of 'N' Battery Royal Horse Artillery From 1st January 1916 To 31st January 1916		
War Diary	St Maxent		
Heading	War Diary Of 'N' Battery Royal Horse Artillery From 1st February 1916 To 29th February 1916		
War Diary	St Maxent	01/02/1916	07/02/1916
War Diary	St Maxent Martainneville	08/02/1916	18/02/1916
War Diary	Vielle Chapelle	19/02/1916	29/02/1916
Heading	War Diary Of 'N' Battery Royal Horse Artillery From 1st March 1916 To 31st March 1916		
War Diary	Vielle Chapelle	01/03/1916	09/03/1916
War Diary	Naours	10/03/1916	15/03/1916
War Diary	Havernas	16/03/1916	31/03/1916
Heading	War Diary Of 'N' Battery Royal Horse Artillery From 1st March 1916 To 31st March 1916		
War Diary	Havernas	01/05/1916	31/05/1916
Heading	War Diary Of 'N' Battery Royal Horse Artillery From 1st June 1916 To 30th June		
War Diary	Acheux	01/06/1916	01/06/1916
War Diary	Allennay	02/06/1916	08/06/1916

War Diary	Acheux	09/06/1916	22/06/1916
War Diary	St Ricquer	23/06/1916	26/06/1916
War Diary	Riencourt	27/06/1916	27/06/1916
War Diary	Bussy Les Daours	28/06/1916	30/06/1916
Heading	War Diary Of 'N' Battery Royal Horse Artillery From 1st July 1916 To 31st July 1916		
War Diary	Bussy-Les-Daours	01/07/1916	12/07/1916
War Diary	Meaulte	13/07/1916	22/07/1916
War Diary	Bussy-Les-Daours	23/07/1916	07/08/1916
War Diary	Allery	08/08/1916	08/08/1916
War Diary	Guimerville	09/08/1916	25/08/1916
War Diary	Ailly-Sur-Somme.	26/08/1916	26/08/1916
War Diary	Frechencourt	27/08/1916	09/09/1916
War Diary	Bussy-Les-Daours	10/09/1916	10/09/1916
War Diary	Near Meault	14/09/1916	14/09/1916
War Diary	Near Fricourt	15/09/1916	16/09/1916
War Diary	Bussy-Les-Daours	17/09/1916	30/09/1916
Heading	War Diary Of 'N' Battery Royal Horse Artillery From 1st October 1916 To 31st October 1916		
War Diary	Bussy-Les-Daours	01/10/1916	05/10/1916
War Diary	In Action	06/10/1916	27/10/1916
War Diary	In Action Or Somme Near High Wood	01/11/1916	09/11/1916
War Diary	Argoeuves	12/11/1916	12/11/1916
War Diary	Metigny	13/11/1916	13/11/1916
War Diary	Beauchamps	14/11/1916	31/12/1916
Heading	2 Ind Cav. Div Secunderabad Bde Signal Troop 1914 Aug To 1916 Dec		
Heading	War Diary Of Signal Troop Secunderabad Brigade From 12 August To 30th November 1914		
War Diary	Bangalore	12/08/1914	29/08/1914
War Diary	Secunderabad	30/08/1914	31/08/1914
War Diary	Bombay	01/09/1914	02/09/1914
War Diary	Indian Ocean	03/09/1914	09/09/1914
War Diary	Gulf Of Aden	10/09/1914	10/09/1914
War Diary	Aden	11/09/1914	11/09/1914
War Diary	Red Sea	12/09/1914	16/09/1914
War Diary	Suez	17/09/1914	17/09/1914
War Diary	Port Said	18/09/1914	18/09/1914
War Diary	Mediterranean	19/09/1914	29/09/1914
War Diary	Marseilles	27/09/1914	06/10/1914
War Diary	Rail	06/10/1914	06/10/1914
War Diary	Orleans	07/10/1914	31/10/1914
Heading	Communications-9th Ind Cav Bde 1st Nov-16th		
War Diary	Vieille Chapelle	01/11/1914	16/11/1914
War Diary	Bethune	17/11/1914	20/11/1914
Miscellaneous			
War Diary	Bethune	21/11/1914	30/11/1914
War Diary	War Diary of Signal Troop Secandrabad Cavalry Brigade From 1st December 1914 To 31st Dec 1915		
War Diary	Bethune	01/12/1914	11/12/1914
War Diary	Chateau Beaulieu-Busnes	11/12/1914	19/12/1914
War Diary	Busnes	19/12/1914	21/12/1914
War Diary	Rue De Bethune	21/12/1914	28/12/1914
War Diary	Communications Of Secunderabad Cavalry Brigade		
War Diary	Le Berques	29/12/1914	31/12/1914

Miscellaneous	War Diary Of Signal Troop, Secunderabad Cavalry Brigade From 1st January 1915 To 31st May 1915		
War Diary	Isbergues	01/01/1915	03/03/1915
War Diary	Allouagne	11/03/1915	14/03/1915
War Diary	Diagram Of Communications In Area Therouanne-Marthes-Mametz		
War Diary	Mametz	16/03/1915	28/04/1915
War Diary	1 Mile S.W. Of Proven	28/04/1915	06/05/1915
Miscellaneous	Diagram Of Communications Area Bomy-Cuhem Laires		
War Diary	Bomy	07/05/1915	31/05/1915
Heading	War Diary Of Signal Troop Secunderabad Cavalry Brigade From 1st August 1915 To 30th September 1915		
War Diary		01/08/1915	12/08/1915
War Diary			
War Diary		13/08/1915	30/09/1915
Heading	Sketch Plan Of Authville		
Heading	War Diary Of Secunderabad Cavalry Brigade Signal Troop From 1st October 1915 To 31st October 1915		
War Diary	Fienvillers	01/10/1915	14/10/1915
War Diary	Ribeaucourt	14/10/1915	22/10/1915
War Diary	Pont-Remy.	22/10/1915	29/10/1915
War Diary			
Miscellaneous	To The Officers Commanding All Units. Secunderabad Cavalry Brigade.	23/10/1915	23/10/1915
Miscellaneous	Orders For Relay Post.		
Heading	War Diary Of Signal Troop, Secunderabad Cavalry Brigade From 1st November 1915 To 31st		
War Diary		01/11/1915	07/11/1915
War Diary		19/11/1915	30/11/1915
Miscellaneous	Communications Secunderabad Cavalry Brigade November 1915.		
War Diary	Caumont	01/12/1915	16/12/1915
War Diary		11/12/1915	31/12/1915
War Diary	Communications Secunderabad Cavalry Brigade.		
War Diary	Caumont	01/01/1916	31/01/1916
War Diary		29/01/1916	31/01/1916
Miscellaneous	Communications Secunderabad Cavalry Brigade		
Heading	War Diary Of Signal Troop Secunderabad Cavalry Brigade From 1st February 1916 To 29th February 1916		
War Diary	Caumont	01/02/1916	03/02/1916
War Diary	Ercourt	08/02/1916	28/02/1916
Miscellaneous	Diagram Of Communications Secunderabad Cavalry Brigade		
Heading	War Diary Of Signal Troop, Secunderabad Cavalry Brigade From 1st March 1916 To 31st March 1916		
War Diary	Ercourt	01/03/1916	31/03/1916
War Diary		30/03/1916	30/03/1916
Heading	War Diary Of Signal Troop Secunderabad Cavalry Brigade From 1st July 1916 To 31st July 1916.		
War Diary		01/07/1916	31/07/1916
Miscellaneous	War Diary Of Signal Troop Secunderabad Cavalry Brigade From 1st August 1916 To 31st August 1916.		
War Diary	Bussy-Les-Daours	01/08/1916	31/08/1916

Heading	War Diary Of Signal Troop Secunderabad Cavalry Brigade From 1st September 1916 To 30th September 1916.		
War Diary	Nesle-Normandeuse.	01/09/1916	29/09/1916
Heading	War Diary Of Signal Troop Secunderabad Cavalry Brigade From 1st October 1916 To 30th November 1916		
War Diary	St Pierre A Gouy	01/10/1916	31/10/1916
Diagram etc	Diagram Of Communications Secunderbad Cav Bde At St Pierre A-Gouy October 1916		
Heading	Signal Troop Sbad Cavy Bde War Diary From 1st November To 31st November 1916 Vol V.		
War Diary	Feuquieres.	01/11/1916	30/11/1916
Diagram etc	Diagram Of Communications Sedbad Cav Bde		
Heading	War Diary Of Signal Troop. Secunderabad Cavalry Brigade From 1st December 1916 To 31st December 1916.		
War Diary	Feuquieres.	01/12/1916	31/12/1916
Heading	BEF 2nd Ind. Cav. Div. Secunderabad Bde Bde Machine Gun Sqd 1916 Feb To 1916 Dec.		
War Diary	Martainneville.	01/03/1916	13/03/1916
War Diary	St Maxent.	08/02/1916	29/02/1916
War Diary		14/03/1916	31/03/1916
Heading	War Diary Of Machine Gun Squadron. Secunderabad Cavalry Brigade From 1st April 1916 To 30th April 1916		
War Diary	Martainneville.	01/04/1916	30/04/1916
Heading	War Diary Of Machine Gun Squadron. Secunderabad Cavalry Brigade From 1st May 1916 To 31st May 1916.		
War Diary	Martainneville-France.	03/05/1916	08/05/1916
War Diary	Canchy.	09/05/1916	14/05/1916
War Diary	Martainneville.	15/05/1916	19/05/1916
War Diary	Rogeant.	20/05/1916	31/05/1916
Heading	War Diary Of Machine Gun Squadron. Secunderabad Cavalry Brigade From 1st June 1916 To 30th June 1916.		
War Diary		01/06/1916	30/06/1916
Heading	War Diary Of Machine Gun Squadron, Secunderabad Cavalry Brigade From 1st July 1916 To 31st July.		
War Diary	Querrieu.	01/07/1916	31/07/1916
Miscellaneous	War Diary Of Machine Gun Squadron, Secunderabad Cavalry Brigade From 1st August 1916 To 31st August 1916.		
War Diary	Querrieu.	01/08/1916	31/08/1916
Miscellaneous	War Diary Of Machine Gun Squadron. Secunderabad Cavalry Brigade From 1st September 1916 To 30th September 1916		
War Diary	Bourbel	01/09/1916	05/09/1916
War Diary	Oissy	06/09/1916	06/09/1916
War Diary	Bussy.	07/09/1916	13/09/1916
War Diary	Meaulte	14/09/1916	14/09/1916
War Diary	Mametz Wood	15/09/1916	16/09/1916
War Diary	Bussy	17/09/1916	25/09/1916
War Diary	Reincourt.	26/09/1916	28/09/1916
War Diary	Gouy	29/09/1916	30/09/1916

Heading	War Diary Of Machine Gun Squadron. Secunderabad Cavalry Brigade From 1st October 1916 To 30th November 1916.		
War Diary	Le Gard.	02/10/1916	31/10/1916
Heading	Machine Gun Squadron Sbad Cavalry Brigade War Diary From 1st November 1916 To 30th November 1916 Vol V.		
War Diary	Le Gard St Pierre-a. Gouy	01/11/1916	30/11/1916
Heading	War Diary Of Machine Gun Squadron, Secunderabad Cavalry Brigade From 1st December 1916 To 31st December 1916.		
War Diary	Buigny-Les-Gamaches.	01/12/1916	31/12/1916
Heading	BEF 2 Ind. Cav. Div. Secunderabad Bde Mobile Vet Section 1914 Oct to 1916 Dec.		
Heading	War Diary Of Mobile Veterinary Section, Secunderabad Cavalry Brigade From 28th October 1914 To. 7th March 1915.		
War Diary	Camp La Source Orleans.	20/10/1914	29/11/1914
War Diary		18/11/1914	19/11/1914
War Diary		20/11/1915	23/11/1915
War Diary	Bethune.		
War Diary	Busnes.	06/12/1915	06/12/1915
War Diary	Pont De Balque.	22/12/1916	22/12/1916
War Diary	Neufpre	07/03/1915	07/03/1915
War Diary	Camp La Source Orleans.	28/10/1914	29/10/1914
War Diary		18/11/1914	19/11/1914
War Diary		20/11/1915	23/11/1915
War Diary	Bethune.		
War Diary	Busnes.	06/12/1915	06/12/1915
War Diary	Pont De Balque.	22/12/1915	22/12/1915
War Diary	Neufpre	07/03/1915	07/03/1915
Heading	War Diary Of Mobile Veterinary Section, Secunderabad Cavalry Brigade From 7th April 1915 To, 30th June 1915.		
War Diary	Neufpre.	07/03/1915	09/05/1915
War Diary	Reclinghem.	10/05/1915	20/05/1915
War Diary	Glem.	21/05/1915	30/06/1915
Heading	War Diary Of Mobile Veterinary Section. Secunderabad Cavalry Brigade From 1st July 1915 To 31st August 1915.		
War Diary	Glem.	01/07/1915	11/07/1915
War Diary	Wandonne.	11/07/1915	01/08/1915
War Diary	Brimieux.	02/08/1915	02/08/1915
War Diary	Bellacourt.	03/08/1915	03/08/1915
War Diary	Crouy	04/08/1915	07/08/1915
War Diary	Soues.	08/08/1915	31/08/1915
Heading	War Diary Of Mobile Veterinary Section Secunderabad Cavalry Brigade From 1st October 1915 To 31st October 1915.		
War Diary	Soues.	01/09/1915	21/09/1915
War Diary	Gorges.	22/09/1915	12/10/1915
War Diary	Bussus Bussue.	13/10/1915	22/10/1915
War Diary	Pont Remy.	23/10/1915	31/10/1915
Heading	War Diary Of Mobile Veterinary Section, Secunderabad Cavalry Brigade From 1st November 1915 To 30th November 1915.		

War Diary	Pont Remy.	01/11/1915	06/11/1915
War Diary	St Muxent.	06/11/1915	20/11/1915
War Diary	Limeux.	21/11/1915	30/11/1915
Heading	War Diary Of Mobile Veterinary Section, Secunderabad Cavalry Brigade From 1st December 1915 To 31st December 1915.		
War Diary	Limeux.	01/12/1915	17/12/1915
War Diary	Huppy.	18/12/1915	31/12/1915
Heading	War Diary Of Mobile Section. Secunderabad Cavalry Brigade From 1st January 1916 To 31st January 1916.		
War Diary	Huppy.	01/01/1916	31/01/1916
Heading	War Diary Of Mobile Veterinary Section. Secunderabad Cavalry Brigade From 1st February 1916 To 31st March 1916.		
War Diary	Huppy.	01/02/1916	03/02/1916
War Diary	Ercourt.	03/02/1916	31/03/1916
Heading	War Diary Of Mobile Veterinary Section. Secunderabad Cavalry Brigade From 1st April 1916 To 30th April 1916.		
War Diary	Ercourt.	01/04/1916	20/04/1916
War Diary	St Riquier.	20/04/1916	29/04/1916
War Diary	Ercourt.	30/04/1916	30/04/1916
Heading	War Diary Of Mobile Veterinary Section. Secunderabad Cavy Brigade From 1st May 1916 To 31st August 1916.		
War Diary	Ercourt.	01/05/1916	22/06/1916
War Diary	St Riquier.	22/06/1916	27/06/1916
War Diary	Bussy Les Daours.	28/06/1916	13/07/1916
War Diary	Meanlt Bray Monlabain Valley.	13/07/1916	15/07/1916
War Diary	Meanlt.	16/07/1916	23/07/1916
War Diary	Burry.	23/07/1916	31/07/1916
War Diary	Burry Les Daours	01/08/1916	07/08/1916
War Diary	Burry.	08/08/1916	08/08/1916
War Diary	Airaines.	09/08/1916	09/08/1916
War Diary	Nesle Normandeuse	10/08/1916	16/08/1916
War Diary	Riencourt.	17/08/1916	17/08/1916
War Diary	Burry Les Daours	18/08/1916	30/08/1916
Heading	War Diary Of Mobile Veterinary Section Secunderabad Cavalry Brigade From 1st September 1916 To 30th September 1916.		
War Diary	Nestle Normandeuse.	01/09/1916	06/09/1916
War Diary	Oissy.	07/09/1916	08/09/1916
War Diary	Bussy-Les-Daours.	08/09/1916	15/09/1916
War Diary	Albert.	16/09/1916	17/09/1916
War Diary	Bussy-Les-Daours.	18/09/1916	26/09/1916
War Diary	Oissy.	27/09/1916	30/09/1916
Heading	War Diary Of Mobile Veterinary Section, Secunderabad Veterinary Brigade From 1st October 1916 To 30th November 1916.		
War Diary	St Pierre A Gouy.	01/10/1916	01/11/1916
War Diary	Feuquieres.	02/11/1916	30/11/1916
Heading	War Diary Of Mobile Veterinary Section, Secunderabad Veterinary Brigade From 1st December 1916 To 31st December 1916.		
War Diary	Feuquieres	01/12/1916	31/12/1916

B.E.F. FRANCE & FLANDERS.
2 INDIAN CAV DIVISION.
SECUNDERABAD CAV BRIGADE
'N' BTY ROYAL HORSE ARTILLERY
1914 AUG TO 1916 DEC.
BRIGADE SIGNAL TROOP.
1914 AUG TO 1916 DEC.
BDE MACHINE GUN SQUADRON
1916 FEB TO 1916 DEC.
MOBILE VETERINARY SECTION
1914 OCT TO 1916 DEC.

1188

B.E.F. FRANCE & FLANDERS.
2 INDIAN CAV DIVISION.
SECUNDERABAD CAV BRIGA[DE]
'N' BTY ROYAL HORSE ART
1914 AUG TO 1916 DEC.
BRIGADE SIGNAL TROOP.
1914 AUG TO 1916 DEC.
BDE MACHINE GUN SQUADRO[N]
1916 FEB TO 1916 DEC.
MOBILE VETERINARY SEC
1914 OCT TO 1916 DEC.

1188

BEF

2 IND. CAV. DIV

SECUNDERABAD BDE

"N" BTY. RHA

1914 AUG - 1916 DEC

Secunderabad
2nd Ind Cav.

War Diary 121/4046
of
"N" Battery R.H.A.
From 9-8-14
To 31-12-14
Volume I
Pp 1 to 5

Army Form C. 2118.

WAR DIARY

INTELLIGENCE SUMMARY.

(Erase heading not required.)

Instructions regarding War Diaries and Intelligence Summaries are contained in F. S. Regs., Part II, and the Staff Manual respectively. Title pages will be prepared in manuscript.

Hour, Date, Place.	Summary of Events and Information.	Remarks and references to Appendices
10.pm August 5. Trimulghury	Order to mobilise received from G.O.C. 9th Secunderabad Division.	
6.am July 10th	Started mobilising.	
6.am " 14th	Horses + men arrived from Mhow + Bangalore also 3 majors.	
9.am " 15th	Inspected by G.O.C. 9th Cavalry Brigade.	
6.am " 26th Bangalore	Inspected by G.O.C. 9th Division.	
12 noon " 30. Trimulghury	Orders to entrain Aug 31st at noon.	
— " 31st Secunderabad	Entrained + started for Port of Embarkation 2 trains 280 rank file each.	
6.30 Sept 1st Bombay	Detained food destitution no bread for troops.	
12 noon — 2nd "	Embarked on S.S. Via. Left dock at 4 pm arrived in stream	
12 noon — 3rd "	Sailed N°4 transport convoyed by H.M.S. Dartmouth.	
9.am "		
5.am " 11th Aden	Arrived outside change escorts to Northbrook 9 pm Prim	
5.am " 12th Red Sea	One horse died. Heart failure (Syncope)	
10.pm " 14th "	H.m.s. Black Prince joined escort.	
9.pm " 17th Suez	Entered Canal 11 pm reported destination ALEXANDRIA.	
12 noon " 18th Port Said.	Arrived Vould. One horse died colic (sand) 4th Canal & sailed 9 pm.	
6pm " 19th in Levant.	Met convoy of 16 transports from Alexandria + Cruiser Weymouth	
12 noon " 22nd off Malta	Passed	

Army Form C. 2118.

WAR DIARY
or
INTELLIGENCE SUMMARY.

(Erase heading not required.)

Instructions regarding War Diaries and Intelligence Summaries are contained in F.S. Regs., Part II, and the Staff Manual respectively. Title pages will be prepared in manuscript.

Hour, Date, Place.	Summary of Events and Information.	Remarks and references to Appendices
2.30pm Sept. 26th Marseilles	Went inside Roadsted and dropped anchor.	
10 am 29th "	Disembarked 4 pm marched to Camp La Penne 2 miles	
5 am Oct. 5th "	Entrained. Left at 10.45.	
3 pm Oct. 7th Orleans.	Arrived disentrained marched to Camp La Source 6 miles	
" 22nd " "	O.C. Civ: Ride left on to Arras	
" 30th " "	Entrained for the front.	
5.30pm " 31st "		L/Cpl Mays RHA
9.6am Nov 1st Rupnette	Detrained marched to St Venant avec blessés + skills to rebels	Gnr W Melton RHA
10 am " 2nd "	Brigade in dismounted action. Swanston killed	Gnr G W Seemer sent to 1st Heavy Squadron
6 am " 5th Pont du Hem	Marched out dug pits came into action against German trenches	in its Brigade Short Re
6 " "	Three log slowitzer firing. Heavy firing at night in mink etc	Major Roston to 1st Div W. of 15
1 " " "	Foggy later fine Searched Pits to rules tall on line Supplement from	Lieut Harris ~ Major Oct 30
		Lieut Carlisle ~ Capt
		" Kynaston ~ "
		" Adam ~ "
		" Rouse

WAR DIARY or INTELLIGENCE SUMMARY

Army Form C. 2118.

(Erase heading not required.)

Hour, Date, Place.	Summary of Events and Information.	Remarks and references to Appendices
Nov 8th 1914.		
4pm Pont du Hem	Fired at German trenches. German aeroplanes. Quiet day.	
12 noon Nov 9th "	Heavy firing on left. Otherwise quiet day.	
" 10th " "	Fired in front of Seaforth trenches. Capt Hutchison in Tournai	
3 pm " " "	Fired for 10 min rapid at 3 + 3.45 p.m. Trees-Rouge-Bois-Nbg	
1 pm " 11th "	12 m. to 12.45 am. to assist attack by 5th Infant Brigade	
6 am " 12th "	Fired to locate German machine + telescope located German	Fall of Kiau Chau
	about moved to Levrentie. Reconnoitred round district	
12 noon " 13th Sailly	no 20 mm. Ridiculed snare. Agt to recruit CRA.	
	Orders to remain at Sailly. 1 pm orders to return to Pont du Hem	
6 am " 14th Pont du Hem	marched 1.30. Returned to B.d. CRA.	
	Shelled German Battery which scored 2 hits. First army	
Nov 15 " — "	orders to myself. Orders to remain. Intense to mort	of 8th Division Artillery command
7.30 am " 16th Pont Tournant	marched to Pont Tournant reconnoitred 19th Battery's position	
	+ Sherming Station.	
5 am 17th Richebourg	Harvey + Ritchelmig got line of German trenches misty.	
9 am 18th "	Got + trier to harry fun Ohio also range force in am.	
9.30 pm 19th "	Snow + hail. Front saw no activity in enemy's lines	
9 am 20th "	Frost 12.0 Saw a few Germans.	
9 am 21st "	Reconnoitred alternative position from Chateau Waterlopp.	
9 am 22nd "	Quiet day.	
11 am 23rd "	Enemy fired bunch of 30 Pitrines rounds attacked at night. Fired 3/6 rounds	

Army Form C. 2118.

WAR DIARY
or
INTELLIGENCE SUMMARY.
(Erase heading not required.)

Instructions regarding War Diaries and Intelligence Summaries are contained in F. S. Regs., Part II, and the Staff Manual respectively. Title pages will be prepared in manuscript.

Hour, Date, Place.	Summary of Events and Information.	Remarks and references to Appendices
4 a.m. Nov: 24th Rotembourg	Counter attack of Shamrock successful 100 prisoners. Quiet in front. Thenul.	
12 noon - 25th -	B.S.M. Brown billet from front mortar wound.	
- 26th -	Enveloped in snow. Enemy's aeroplane did some pretty shooting.	
6 a.m. -	New Commander R.A. Jordan D.S.O. got line to 15th Sikhs	
7 a.m. 27th -	Sent off reconnoitre 3rd Aviation. 3 p.m. sent to reconnoitre 4. Aviation	
3 p.m. 28th -	To observe Carbide to dig. Nutmeg to Marmalade. Limit for knife man avectre	
29th -	Sent up German Supply dump at 8 a.m. + 9 p.m.	
7 a.m. 30th -	Shelled German Battery which creeping. Shelled maneuver in Tapine	
1.30 a.m. Dec 1st Hinges	Tractor Am. Col. 43 - 2nd Battery. True position + orientation Station	
2nd Aurelette	Desultary shelling. Days on Service of German activity.	
3rd -	Hamlet own to 93rd Battery, moved to Aurelette	
	1 Sect. Paraded for inspection by H.M. King GEORGE V.	
	Resting.	
	do.	

H.K. Cotton, Lieut-Colonel RHA.
Comdr. N. Battery RHA.

WAR DIARY
or
INTELLIGENCE SUMMARY.

(Erase heading not required.)

Army Form C. 2118.

ADJUTANT GENERAL
10. JAN. 1915
BASE OFFICE

Instructions regarding War Diaries and Intelligence Summaries are contained in F. S. Regs., Part II, and the Staff Manual respectively. Title pages will be prepared in manuscript.

Hour, Date, Place.	Summary of Events and Information.	Remarks and references to Appendices
11.am. Dec: 7th 1914. AVELETTE	Inspected by Sir James McCaw, Comd: Force.	
" 10th "	Lt Col Rotton proceed on 7 days leave.	
" 14th "	Centre Section into action close to GIVENCHY under 2 A.M. ORD DIVISION 17th & 6th ENTRENCH: Wounded + 3 men killed & wounded
" 19th "	Right Section relieved Centre Section.	
10.am. Dec 20. LE TOURET	Centre + Left Sections into action at LE TOURET. Supported attack by the	Both detachments heavily engaged day and night.
21st " "	" " " " supported attack by 2nd Div.	" " " "
22nd " "	" " " Centre working party by the all night.	" " " "
23rd " "	" " " Centre relief by GURDS 1st Brigade.	" " " "
24th " "	Right Section relieved by R.A. 1st Div. Centre + Left Stopped GERMAN attacks	Comenced action 1.30pm.
25th " "	CHRISTMAS DAY. Last firing.	
26th " "	Relieved by R.A. 2nd DIVISION. marched to LA TOUPIE.	
27 F. LA TOUPIE	In billets minihunders guns and equipment.	
28th " "		
29th " "		
30th " "		
31st " "		

J.C. Rotton Lieut-Colonel R.H.A.
Comd.s. N Battery R.H.A.

Excellent work rendered highly
5/16
2/1

121/4401

WAR DIARY
OF
"N" Battery R.H.A.

From 1st January 1915 TO 31st January 1915.

WAR DIARY

"N" BATTERY, R.H.A.

Army Form C. 2118.

No 3 Section
A.G's Office at Base
I.E. Force
Passed to S. Sect.
on 8 — 2 — 15

ADJUTANT GENERAL, INDIA
-8. FEB. 1915
BASE OFFICE

Instructions regarding War Diaries and Intelligence Summaries are contained in F. S. Regs., Part II, and the Staff Manual respectively. Title pages will be prepared in manuscript.

(Erase heading not required.)

Hour, Date, Place.		Summary of Events and Information.	Remarks and references to Appendices
LA ROUPIE.	Jan. 1st 1915	Conditioning of horses. Instructions to Telephone Party.	
	" 2nd	" " Reconnaissance & Gun Drill Classes.	
	" 3rd	Service at ISBERGUES 15 May for success of Allies.	
	" 4th to Jan. 10th	Conditioning of Horses. Reconnaissance & Telephone Classes. Repair of Carriages & Gun Drill.	
10.15 am	Jan. 11th	Inspection by G.O.C. 2nd Indian Cavalry Division.	
		J.S. marching order & all transport loaded.	
	Jan 12th	Conditioning of Horses. Draft of 30 men joined Battery. 2nd Lt. A.G. Herr joined on appointment to R.H.A.	
	Jan 13th	Conditioning of Horses. Transport parade under Bde. Transport Officer.	
9 am	Jan. 14th	S'brd Cavalry Bde. Route March with loaded transport.	
	Jan. 15th	Conditioning of Horses. 2nd Lt. C.H. Cameron joined on appointment to R.H.A.	
	Jan 16th	Conditioning of Horses. Gun Drill Instructions to Draft.	

Army Form C. 2118.

WAR DIARY
INTELLIGENCE SUMMARY
"N" BATTERY. R.H.A.

(Erase heading not required.)

Instructions regarding War Diaries and Intelligence Summaries are contained in F.S. Regs., Part II, and the Staff Manual respectively. Title pages will be prepared in manuscript.

Hour, Date, Place.	Summary of Events and Information.	Remarks and references to Appendices
LA ROUPIE Jan 17th	Service. Sgt Woods & Stone promoted RSM. & BQMS. Sgt Spain promoted RQMS & posted to G. Amm Col.	
Jan 18th	Lt. Col. J.G. Bitton & Major O.M. Harris posted to Home Establishment. Ordered to join at once. Capt. A.O. Hutchison posted to 37th Batt. R.H.A. Ordered to join.	
7.30 am	Cavalry Corps concentration at ENQUIN. For inspection by Sir John French. C-in-C. "N" Battery marched with 5th Cavl Bde from Arie. Snow. Very cold.	
Jan 19th	Cinditioning of Horses. Gun Drill.	
Jan 20th	Conditioning of Horses. Reconnaissance class. Gun Drill. Instructions to last Dept.	
Jan 23rd	Battery Gun Drill. Conditioning of Horses. Reconnaisance Class & NCOs in care of Equipment.	
Jan 25th	Major A.H.D. West appointed to command N Battery & joined.	

Army Form O. 2118.

WAR DIARY
or
INTELLIGENCE SUMMARY.

"N" BATTERY R.H.A.

(Erase heading not required.)

Instructions regarding War Diaries and Intelligence Summaries are contained in F. S. Regs., Part II, and the Staff Manual respectively. Title pages will be prepared in manuscript.

Hour, Date, Place.	Summary of Events and Information.	Remarks and references to Appendices
LA ROUPIE. Jan 26th	Battery Gun Drill. Exercising of horses. Reconnaissance Soft Surfaces.	
Jan 27th	I.S. Marching Order. 5th Bde Tactical exercise.	
Jan 28th	Conditioning of horses. Telephone + Reconnaissance instruments.	
	I.S. Marching Order parade for to with the S'toof Cavalry	
	Brigade for inspection by G.O.C. Indian Cavalry Corps.	
Jan 29th	Gun Drill. Exercising horses. Capt. R.F. Adam left the	
	Battery on appointing to 31st Division. —	
Jan 30th	Conditioning of horses. Telephone party scheme.	
Jan 31st	Sunday. Under orders to move at 2 hours notice since	
	12. midnight. 29/30/31.	

J. West.
Major R.H.A.
Commanding N. Battery R.H.A.

Serial No. 221.

12/4/19

WAR DIARY

"I" Battery R.H.A.

From 1st February 1915 to 28th February 1915

Army Form C. 2118.

WAR DIARY

or

INTELLIGENCE SUMMARY.

"N" Battery R.H.A.

(Erase heading not required.)

Instructions regarding War Diaries and Intelligence Summaries are contained in F. S. Regs., Part II, and the Staff Manual respectively. Title pages will be prepared in manuscript.

Hour, Date, Place.	Summary of Events and Information.	Remarks and references to Appendices
LA ROUPIE —		
Feb 1st to 28th	Battery remained in Billets at LA ROUPIE. Battery training in all departments was carried out and occasional days were devoted to training with the Brigade & Division.	
Feb 11th	At a tactical exercise of the Secunderabad Cav. Brigade H.R.H. the Prince of Wales paid a visit and watched the work of the troops.	
Feb. 6th	2 Lieut A.G. Hess temporarily transferred to 103rd Bty R.F.A. 2 Lieut A.L. Kennedy from 103rd Bty R.F.A. temporarily attached to "N" R.H.A.	

J.M Airlie Capt RHA
for O.C. "N" Battery RHA.

— 6. MAR 1915

121/5114

WAR DIARY
"N" Battery R.H.A.

From 1st March 1915 to 31st March 1915

Army Form C. 2118.

WAR DIARY
or
INTELLIGENCE SUMMARY.

"N" BATTERY R.H.A.

(Erase heading not required.)

Instructions regarding War Diaries and Intelligence Summaries are contained in F.S. Regs., Part II, and the Staff Manual respectively. Title pages will be prepared in manuscript.

[Stamp: ADJUTANT GENERAL INDIA — 5 APR 1915 — 1144 W.D — BASE OFFICE]

Hour, Date, Place.	Summary of Events and Information.	Remarks and references to Appendices
LA ROUPIE March 1st & 2nd	In billets at LA ROUPIE.	
3rd	Marched 2.0 a.m. to billets & bivouac 1½ miles NE of MERVILLE with rest of artillery of 2nd I.D. Batteries detached to 8th Infantry Division & grouped under Lt-Col Ostwith R.H.A. with 29th & 35th Bdes R.F.A.	Intimation that Lieut O.B. Nus of the Battery killed in action with 107th Battery R.F.A. near YPRES on 24-2-15.
PONT DU HEM 4th	Marched 1.0 a.m. to PONT DU HEM & occupied position before daylight just E of the ESTAIRES—LA BASSEE road about 50 yards SE of the cross roads at PONT DU HEM.	
5th	Horses returned to billets near MERVILLE. Entrenching carried on with Battery registered and points it's one allotted it. (Fired 14 rounds).	Cpls Evans & Banks names appeared in orders as awarded D.C.M.
6th	Carried on entrenching. Quiet day.	
7th	Battery fired 19 rounds registering points.	
8th	Fired 14 rounds registering points.	
9th	Fired 18 rounds registering points.	
PONT DU HEM March 10th	General attack by 4th Corps & Indian Corps on German positions. Objective:—(1) Capture of NEUVE CHAPELLE. (2) Occupation of the line AUBERS, LEPLOUICH, LA-CLIQUETERIE FERME, LIGNY DE GRAND.	
7-30 am	German position held by German 7th Corps. Intense bombardment of enemies position by all Batteries. Tasks & times previously allotted to each Battery. Task for "N" Battery R.H.A. as follows:—	

[Signature]

Army Form C. 2118.

WAR DIARY
of
INTELLIGENCE SUMMARY.

"N" BATTERY R.H.A.

Instructions regarding War Diaries and Intelligence Summaries are contained in F.S. Regs., Part II, and the Staff Manual respectively. Title pages will be prepared in manuscript.

(Erase heading not required.)

Hour, Date, Place.	Summary of Events and Information.	Remarks and references to Appendices
PONT DU HEM		
March 10th 7.40am to 8.50am	An area of the German support trenches on the northern edge of NEUVE CHAPELLE. (30 rounds per gun). Range 2500 yds	
8.50am to 8.35am	To search 400 yards on a frontage of 100 yards on N.E. side of NEUVE CHAPELLE. (10 rounds per gun). Range 2600—3000 yds	
8.35 am	To watch with a steady rate of fire an area of ground E of NEUVE CHAPELLE. Range 3000 yds.	
8-8.36 am	This programme was strictly adhered to.	
	The Infantry assault commenced. German guns remained inactive.	
10.50 am	Orders received to keep left of fire 400 yards E of NEUVE CHAPELLE	
12-15 pm	Orders to sweep area E of orchard on N edge of NEUVE CHAPELLE — 10 rounds per gun. Range 2700 yards	
3.25 pm	Orders to reconnoitre position further forward to support possible further advance of 8" Division towards line PIETRE — LA RUSSIE. Teams had previously been ordered to be in readiness near PONT DU HEM cross roads.	
6-0 pm	Position selected about 1 mile S, and just E of the LA BASSEE road. Battery occupied new position. Position entrenched during night. Expenditure of ammunition 686 rounds. Infantry attack continued. Observation officers with Infantry reported on situation and orders as to fire were issued to Batteries accordingly.	
March 11th		

Army Form C. 2118.

WAR DIARY

"N" BATTERY R.H.A.

INTELLIGENCE SUMMARY.

(Erase heading not required.)

Instructions regarding War Diaries and Intelligence Summaries are contained in F. S. Regs., Part II, and the Staff Manual respectively. Title pages will be prepared in manuscript.

Hour, Date, Place.	Summary of Events and Information.	Remarks and references to Appendices
March 11th 12-0 noon	Orders to open fire on German counterattack from BOIS DE BIEZ, and later to support an attack on it contemplated by the Rifle Brigade. Range about 2700 yds. During the afternoon the Battery came under heavy fire from German heavy howitzers + field guns. The following casualties were sustained :— Killed – No 15316 Sergt. R. Gray. Wounded – " 34293 " H. Flood. " 17309 " W. Beardsley. " 49187 Gnr. J. Williams. Some minor damage was also caused to equipment by shell fire. Towards nightfall the German fire slackened, but a slow rate of fire was kept up all through the night without ceasing. Above was informed during the night. Expenditure of Ammunition 480 rounds.	
March 12th 3-0 am	Orders received to move back to former position. Teams arrived just before daybreak. As Battery started to limber up a very heavy fire broke out from the whole German front, but the Battery was safely extricated under exceptionally trying conditions + retired to its former position at PONT DU HEM.	
8-45 am	Gideon to open fire on N.E. corner of BOIS DE BIEZ and search back 200 yards. Range about 4000 yds.	

Army Form C. 2118.

WAR DIARY
or
INTELLIGENCE SUMMARY.
(Erase heading not required.)

"N" BATTERY R.H.A.

Instructions regarding War Diaries and Intelligence Summaries are contained in F. S. Regs., Part II, and the Staff Manual respectively. Title pages will be prepared in manuscript.

Hour, Date, Place.	Summary of Events and Information.	Remarks and references to Appendices
March 12th 12.0 noon	Orders to bombard area E of NEUVE CHAPELLE to prepare way for Infantry assault. German howitzers fired at Battery but failed to get range.	
4–6 p.m. NEUVE CHAPELLE	Information that Germans dismoralized and leaving BOIS DE BIEZ hurriedly. Battery ordered to push on to NEUVE CHAPELLE and open fire with all haste. Battery moved rapidly down by sections, and one sections were brought into action by the captured German trenches N.W. of the village where they opened fire at a range of 1200 to 1500 yards— One section was kept in reserve for emergencies a little way back. Fire kept up till dark. Orders received not to fire during night and that Battery would be at disposal of G.O.C. 25th Infantry Brigade next day. Expenditure of Ammunition 438 rounds. Lieut L.N. Cameron was killed about midday while acting as observing officer with G.O.C. 25th Infantry Brigade.	
March 13th 3–0 a.m. PONT DU HEM	Orders received to move back to old position at PONT DU HEM. Battery arrived well before daylight and the Battery was retired under some rifle fire from the front to its old position. During the afternoon the Battery was again engaged firing on various points on the German lines. Expenditure of Ammunition 111 rounds.	

Army Form C. 2118.

WAR DIARY

INTELLIGENCE SUMMARY.

"N" BATTERY R.H.A.

(Erase heading not required.)

Instructions regarding War Diaries and Intelligence Summaries are contained in F. S. Regs., Part II, and the Staff Manual respectively. Title pages will be prepared in manuscript.

Hour, Date, Place.	Summary of Events and Information.	Remarks and references to Appendices
March 14th PONT DU HEM -	Morning quiet as infantry attack now stopped. In afternoon some points were registered. Both observation stations used were heavily shelled.	
March 15th	Expenditure of ammunition 23 rounds.	
" 16th	Quiet day. 7 rounds were fired registering a point. Position reconnoitred a mile E. of LEVANTIE as orders received that Battery was to join 7th Division there.	
1 mile E. of LAVENTIE - 17th	In evening one section withdrawn & relieved by a section of 31st Battery R.F.A.	
" 18th	Battery marched and occupied new position after dusk.	
" 19th	Battery fired 56 rounds registering points. Observation from houses in the RUE TILLELOY.	
" 20th	31 more rounds fired registering. Houses moved to billets 1 mile N. of ESTAIRES from LAVENTIE having come under shell fire at the latter place.	
" 21st	Quiet day.	
" 22nd	In morning fired 17 rounds registering points. In afternoon fired 55 rounds registering fresh points. Observation station shelled.	
" 23rd	Fired 23 rounds registering in afternoon.	
" 24th	Very quiet day. Nothing to record. Capt. T.N. Carlile posted as second Cavalry Division B.E.F.	

Army Form C. 2118.

WAR DIARY
of
INTELLIGENCE SUMMARY.

"N" BATTERY R.H.A.

(Erase heading not required.)

Instructions regarding War Diaries and Intelligence Summaries are contained in F. S. Regs., Part II, and the Staff Manual respectively. Title pages will be prepared in manuscript.

Hour, Date, Place.	Summary of Events and Information.	Remarks and references to Appendices
2 Miles E of LAVENTIE.		
March 25th	Quiet day. Nothing to record.	
26th	Horses changed billets to 1 mile W of ESTAIRES.	
27th	Fired 31 rounds. Capt. S.D. Wilson joined Battery on posting vice Capt. Liddle.	
28th	Quiet day. Lieut. G.A. Simpson joined the Battery on first appointment.	
29th	Nothing to record.	
30th	Nothing to record.	
31st	Nothing to record.	

R. West
Major R.H.A.
Comdg "N" Battery R.H.A.

121/5504

Serial No. 226.

WAR DIARY
OF
"N" Battery R.H.A.

From 1st April 1915 To 30th April 1915

Army Form C. 2118.

WAR DIARY
INTELLIGENCE SUMMARY.
(Erase heading not required.)

Instructions regarding War Diaries and Intelligence Summaries are contained in F.S. Regs., Part II, and the Staff Manual respectively. Title pages will be prepared in manuscript.

"N" BATTERY R.H.A.

Hour, Date, Place.	Summary of Events and Information.	Remarks and references to Appendices
2 miles E. of LAVENTIE		
April 1st	Orders received to rejoin 2nd Indian Cavalry Division	Lieut F.A. Fenton joined on 8-4-1915.
2nd	Battery marched at 2.30 am - being relieved by "T" Battery R.H.A. Marched with "Y" and "X" Batteries to billets with 3rd Ind. Cav. Divn.	Lieut F.S. Anderson joined on 24-4-1915
3rd to 5th NIELLES	Battery at NIELLES south of THÉROUANNE - 28 miles. In Billets.	
6th	Marched to REBECQ, 2 miles E and occupied fresh billets.	
7th to 11th REBECQ	In Billets	
12th	Changed billets to NIELLES	
13th	Back to REBECQ.	
14th to 23rd REBECQ	In Billets.	
24th	Move to fresh billeting area about 5 miles W.S.W. of CASSEL with remainder of Indian Cavalry Corps in evening in support of 2nd Army N of YPRES.	
25th	In billets at L'HEY.	
26th 27th L'HEY	In billets.	
28th		
29th PROVEN	Marched at midday and occupied new billets 15 miles N.E. via HOUTKIRK near PROVEN in BELGIUM. In Billets.	
31st	Batty in billets.	
1-5-1915		

[signature]
MAJOR. R.H.A.
COMMANDING "N" BATTERY. R.H.A.

Serial No 221.

121/5799

WAR DIARY
OF

"N." Battery R.H.A.

From 1st May 1915 To 31st May 1915.

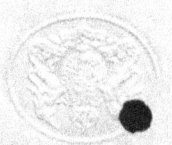

Army Form C. 2118.

WAR DIARY

or INTELLIGENCE SUMMARY.

(Erase heading not required.)

"N" BATTERY R.H.A.

Instructions regarding War Diaries and Intelligence Summaries are contained in F. S. Regs., Part II, and the Staff Manual respectively. Title pages will be prepared in manuscript.

Hour, Date, Place.	Summary of Events and Information.	Remarks and references to Appendices
PROVEN 9 May 1st	Aerets at PROVEN.	
" 2nd	Marched back to L'HEY and occupied billets.	
" 3rd	Marched again at dusk with remainder Artillery of 2nd Ind. Cav. Divn. to join 1st Corps. Marched through the night.	
" 4th	Rested at HAVERSKERQUE for day. In evening marched again. Occupied billets 1 mile E of LOCON early morning. Reconnoitred position for guns near RICHEBOURG St VAAST. Battery attached to Artillery of 1st Infantry Division.	
RICHEBOURG ST VAAST " 5th	Prepared position during day. Occupied it after dusk. 1 horse wounded.	
" 6th	Registered some points and a portion of wire for wire-cutting. Fired 69 rounds.	
" 7th	Wire cutting was registered during day. His rounds fired. Nothing to record.	
" 8th		
" 9th	A lyddite attack by 1st Division on enemy's position was carried out. The attack was preceded by a general bombardment commencing at 5.0 am. The first task of the Battery being to cut wire. This as far as could be seen was very thoroughly done. Fire was then lifted on to enemy's new trench some 50 yards behind first parapet and then an area of ground to the rear was searched to establish a "barrage". The infantry attack broke down under the enemy's machine gun and rifle fire and the retirement of the infantry was carried out under cover of Artillery fire. A deliberate bombardment was now kept up, and gaps in wire were widened.	

Army Form C. 2118.

WAR DIARY
or
INTELLIGENCE SUMMARY.

"N" BATTERY R.H.A.

(Erase heading not required.)

Hour, Date, Place	Summary of Events and Information	Remarks and references to Appendices
May 9th RICHEBOURG St VAAST	A fresh assault was ordered for the afternoon and an intense bombardment was commenced at 2.30. Fire was being all out percussion was fired at the front parapet and when the infantry was well committed the ground in rear of the enemy's parapet was reached. This attack also failed under the German fire and again the infantry stuck under cover of willow fire. No German counter-attack was made, although their artillery was active. The Battery suffered no casualties. Expenditure of ammunition 1152 rounds.	
May 10th	No attack was undertaken. There was some intermittent shelling by the Germans Battery. The Battery fired 30 rounds. Battery did not fire. German artillery fairly active.	
May 11th	Artillery work on both sides only. Battery fired 32 rds.	
May 12th	A deliberate bombardment was kept up all day. In the afternoon the rate of fire was quickened up and then slopped to give damage time to German trenches. The German artillery replied vigorously. During the night the bombardment was kept up intermittently to prevent the enemy's working parties repairing damage. Every effort was made to keep them in a state of uncertainty as to when to expect another attack. At 1–0 am a very lively burst of fire was opened by all	

WAR DIARY
INTELLIGENCE SUMMARY.
(Erase heading not required.)

Army Form C. 2118.

Hour, Date, Place	Summary of Events and Information	Remarks and references to Appendices
May 13th RICHEBOURG St VAAST	Batteries with this Regt. During day and night Battery fired 553 rounds.	
May 14th "	The previous day's programme was repeated as far as we were concerned, bursts of fire being obtained by all Batteries at fixed times, the bombardment being somewhat modified during the night.	
May 15th "	Bombardment again continued all day, the enemy's artillery again replying vigorously. At 11·30 pm our infantry advanced and succeeded in carrying the enemy's trenches near FERME DU BOIS both front and rear trenches. North of this only the 1st trench was carried and south of this there was a section of trench trenches on which the attack did not succeed. Further south again the 7th Divn carried with lines of trenches, while their attack was in progress Batteries searched ground to rear. Our infantry consolidated ground won. A feeble counter attack in morning opposite some CouR D'AvoUE, on to which the fire of Battery was switched, was not pressed. German guns kept up a very vigorous bombardment all day. At 7·0 pm it was very heavy indeed on our support trenches and on RUE DU BOIS, causing our infantry considerable losses. Battery fired 122 rounds on 15th and 16th.	
May 16th "		

WAR DIARY

INTELLIGENCE SUMMARY.

"N" BATTERY R.H.A.

Army Form C. 2118.

Hour, Date, Place	Summary of Events and Information	Remarks and references to Appendices
May 18th RICHEBOURG ST VAAST	A steady bombardment was resumed of all strong points still held by the enemy. A company of German infantry south of FERME DU BOIS surrendered in morning enabling our infantry to link up with the 1st Division. North of the FERME DU BOIS we still held. An attack on FERME DU BOIS in evening failed. Bombardment continued during night. Battery considerably shelled but only one man, Dvr Taylor, very slightly wounded. Total rounds fired 649.	
May 19th "	An intermittent bombardment continued all day. The Guards Brigade attacked FERME COUR D'AVUE at 4.30 pm and made considerable progress. Battery fired 347 rounds. Quieter day. Battery did not fire during day. 24 rounds fired during night.	
May 20th "	Quiet day. Battery fired 91 rounds during night in support of attack by Canadians on our right.	
May 21st "	Battery fired 46 rounds during morning. An attack by the defence Brigade on FERME DU BOIS during night was not successful.	
May 22nd "	Orders were received for the Batteries of 2nd Ind. Cav. Bde. to rejoin their Cavalry Brigades in reserve. The right section was withdrawn during the day to the wagon line being relieved by a section of 3rd Aberdeen Field Battery (Territorial).	

Army Form C. 2118.

WAR DIARY
INTELLIGENCE SUMMARY.
"N" BATTERY R.H.A.

(Erase heading not required.)

Instructions regarding War Diaries and Intelligence Summaries are contained in F.S. Regs., Part II. and the Staff Manual respectively. Title pages will be prepared in manuscript.

Hour, Date, Place	Summary of Events and Information	Remarks and references to Appendices
May 23rd RICHEBOURG ST VAAST	The Centre & Left Sections were withdrawn during the morning back to wagon line.	
May 24th " " "		
May 25th DENNEBROEUCK	Battery marched to billets at DENNEBROEUCK 28 miles West.	
11.15	In Billets overhauling guns & equipment.	

1-6-1915

N.W.
MAJOR R.H.A.
COMDG. "N" BATTERY R.H.A.

Serial No. 221

121/6128

WAR DIARY
OF

"N" Battery R.H.A.

From 1st June 1915. To 30th June 1915.

Army Form C. 2118.

WAR DIARY

~~INTELLIGENCE~~ SUMMARY.
(Erase heading not required.)

"N" BATTERY R.H.A.

JUNE, 1915.

Hour, Date, Place	Summary of Events and Information	Remarks and references to Appendices
June 1 – 30	Nothing to record. Battery in billets at DENNEBROEUCQ.	

J. Jones Major
Commanding "N" By. R.H.A.

Serial. No. 221.

121/6502

WAR DIARY
OF

"N" Battery R.H.A.

FROM 1st July 1915 TO 31st July 1915

Army Form C. 2118.

WAR DIARY
INTELLIGENCE SUMMARY.
(Erase heading not required.)

"N" BATTERY R.H.A.

Hour, Date, Place	Summary of Events and Information	Remarks and references to Appendices
JULY 1st DENNEBROEUCK	In billets at DENNEBROEUCK.	
" 5th	Lieut G.M.C. MARTIN. seconded temporarily for duty with French Munitions.	
" 6th	Inspection by Field-Marshal Lord Kitchener and Sir John French with parts of Indian Cavalry Corps.	
" 10th	Moved billets to RADINGHEM.	
" 10th to 31st	At RADINGHEM.	
" 30th 7.30pm	Orders received to [...] travel to [...] at [...] on 1st August.	

A. W. [signature]
MAJOR R.H.A.
Comdg. "N" BATTERY R.H.A.

Serial No 221.

121/6948

WAR DIARY

OF

"N" Battery R.H.A.

From 1st August 1915 To 31st August 1915

Army Form C. 2118.

WAR DIARY
or
INTELLIGENCE SUMMARY.
(Erase heading not required.)

"N" BATTERY R.H.A.

Instructions regarding War Diaries and Intelligence Summaries are contained in F.S. Regs., Part II. and the Staff Manual respectively. Title pages will be prepared in manuscript.

Hour, Date, Place	Summary of Events and Information	Remarks and references to Appendices
August 1st	2nd Indian Cavalry Division marched to join 3rd Army in Amiens District. Nothing to MAREMIA on River CANCHE 15 miles south west.	
2nd	Marched via ABBEVILLE to MONFLIERES (3) miles south east – about 35 miles.	
3rd	Marched about 15 miles south east. Billeted at BICHECOURT FERME between SOVES and HANGEST.	
4th to 6th inclusive	Sn. Bivouac at BICHECOURT FERME.	
7th	Changed billets to SOVES.	
7th to 13th	In billets at SOVES.	
14th	Marched 8·0 p.m. to CONTAY 23 miles N.E.	
14th	CONTAY. Position reconnoitred. Infantries & Divisional Batteries (T.F.) in occupation. Position originally occupied by French Batteries in Sept 1914 between MARTINSART and MESNIL on the edge of BOIS D'AVELUY.	
15th	RFI. Section occupied position after dark.	
16th	RFI. Section fired 20 rounds registering. 7ms allotted to Battery viz – A ground in front of Leandwahar Brigade, i.e. from River ANCRE near ST PIERRE-DIVION to opposite CHÂTEAU of THIEPVAL. No. 2 and 3 Sections moved in after dark. Horse lines remaining at CONTAY, 9 miles distant...	

[Stamp: A.B. OFFICE AT THE BASE 20 SEP 1915 INDIAN SECTION]

Forms/C. 2118/10

Army Form C. 2118

WAR DIARY
INTELLIGENCE SUMMARY.
(Erase heading not required.)

"N" BATTERY R.H.A.

Instructions regarding War Diaries and Intelligence Summaries are contained in F. S. Regs., Part II. and the Staff Manual respectively. Title pages will be prepared in manuscript.

Hour, Date, Place	Summary of Events and Information	Remarks and references to Appendices
AUGUST 17th	Fired 10 rounds registering. Average range to German front line trenches 3,700 yards. Germans very quiet. Only a little intermittent shelling and sniping.	Sect 2/L.T.W. Ring R.F.A. attached for duty on 16.8.16.
18th	20 rounds fired. A.S.M. Litvin and L/S James left for base.	
	Heavy enemy bombardment on Richts.	
19th	23 rounds fired.	
20th	9 rounds fired	
21st	8 rounds fired	
22nd	Nothing Special	
23rd	21 rounds fired	
24th	20 " "	
25th	10 " "	
26th	13 " "	
27th	5 " "	
28th	15 " "	
29th	35 " " Lieut F.G.E. Mallam rejoined unit from duty with Trench Howitzers.	
30th	7 " "	
31st	13 " "	

R.W.
Major, R.H.
Commanding "N" Battery, R.H.A.

121/7286

Serial No. 221.

WAR DIARY

OF

"N" Battery R.H.A.

From 1st September 1915 To 30th September 1915

WAR DIARY
or
INTELLIGENCE SUMMARY.

(Erase heading not required.)

"N" BATTERY R.H.A. SEPTEMBER 1915

Army Form C. 2118.

Hour, Date, Place	Summary of Events and Information	Remarks and references to Appendices
SEPT 1st IN ACTION near MESNIL	Fired 8 rounds	
2nd	Fired 9 rounds	
3rd	Fired 16 rounds	
4th	Fired 6 rounds	
5th	Nothing Special to report	
6th	Fired 7 rounds	
7th	Fired 11 rounds	
8th	Fired 15 rounds	
9th	Fired 7 rounds	
10th	Fired 7 rounds	
11th	Fired 29 rounds, partly with aeroplane observation	
12th	Fired 28 rounds	
13th	Nothing Special	
14th	Fired 16 rounds. My 2nd Section relieved by section of A100 Battery. Section of D100 Battery also occupied positions on our left.	
15th	Fired 43 rounds. Nos 1 and 3 sections relieved and marched out after dark 15 miles south to St. GRATIEN. Marched at dawn 24 miles back to LE MESRE.	
16th LE MESRE	In Billets at LE MESRE, training in field manoeuvres.	
" to 21st	Inspection by Lord Kitchener of the Indian Cavalry Corps.	
22nd	Marched 20 miles N.E. to GORGES.	
23rd to 30th	In billets at GORGES, under orders to be ready to move at short notice.	

Albert
Commdg "N" Battery
Major R.H.A.
R.H.A.

Serial No. 221.

Confidential

12/7601

War Diary

of

"N" Battery, R.H.A.

FROM 1st October 1915. TO 31st October 1915.

CR/ 29/6/15
26/11/15

Army Form C. 2118

WAR DIARY
INTELLIGENCE SUMMARY

"N" BATTERY R.H.A.

(Erase heading not required.)

Instructions regarding War Diaries and Intelligence Summaries are contained in F. S. Regs., Part II. and the Staff Manual respectively. Title Pages will be prepared in manuscript.

Place	Date	Hour	Summary of Events and Information	Remarks and references to Appendices
GORGES	Oct 1st to 9th inclusive		In billets, under orders to be ready to move at short notice.	
FRANQUEVILLE	10th		Changed billets to FRANQUEVILLE 6 miles west.	
	11th		In billets at FRANQUEVILLE. Divisional Field day	
	12th			
	13th		Moved billets 6 miles West to BUSSUS.	
BUSSUS	13th to 21st inclusive		In billets at BUSSUS.	
	22nd		Moved billets 17 miles S.W. to VAUX MARQUENNEVILLE	
	24th		Moved billets 3 miles N.W. to ST MAXENT EN VIMEUX.	
ST MAXENT EN VIMEUX	24th to 31st inclusive		In billets at St MAXENT EN VIMEUX	

31-10-1915

[signature]
Capt R.H.A.
Comdg "N" Battery R.H.A.

SERIAL No. 221.

Confidential
War Diary

of

"N" Battery, Royal Horse Artillery.

FROM 1st November 1916 TO 30th November 1916

WAR DIARY

INTELLIGENCE SUMMARY

"N" BATTERY R.H.A.

NOVEMBER 1915.

Army Form C.2118

Ind Cav. "N" Battery R.H.A.

Place	Date	Hour	Summary of Events and Information	Remarks and references to Appendices
ST. MAXENT EN VIMEU	Nov 1st		In Billets at ST MAXENT EN VIMEU.	
	11		2nd Lieut A.E. Mitchell R.F.A attached for duty.	
	18		2nd Lieut J. Mellaby R.F.A (attached) transferred to Div'l Amm" Col, 2nd Indian Cavalry Div'n.	

A. W. S
Major R.H.A.
Comdg "N" Battery R.H.A.

SERIAL No 221.

Confidential
War Diary
of

"N" Battery, Royal Horse Artillery.

FROM 1st December 1915 TO 31st December 1915.

Army Form C. 2118

WAR DIARY
INTELLIGENCE SUMMARY
(Erase heading not required.)

"N" Battery R.H.A.

DECEMBER 1915

Place	Date	Hour	Summary of Events and Information	Remarks and references to Appendices
ST MAXENT EN VIMEU	DEC 1st		IN Billets at St MAXENT.	
	10		CAPT. D.C. WILSON R.H.A. Transferred to "L" Battery, 78th Brigade R.F.A, 17th Division.	
	17		LIEUT. G.N.C. MARTIN R.H.A. appointed Temporary Captain	
	31.		IN Billets at ST MAXENT.	

J. Wi──
Comdg. Major R.H.A.
"N" Battery R.H.A.

SERIAL NO. 221.

Confidential

War Diary

of

"N" Battery, Royal Horse Artillery

FROM 1st January 1916 TO 31st January 1916

Army Form C. 2118

WAR DIARY

~~INTELLIGENCE SUMMARY~~

(Erase heading not required.)

"N" BATTERY R.H.A.   JANUARY 1916.

Instructions regarding War Diaries and Intelligence Summaries are contained in F.S. Regs., Part II. and the Staff Manual respectively. Title Pages will be prepared in manuscript.

Place	Date	Hour	Summary of Events and Information	Remarks and references to Appendices
ST. MAXENT	1916. JANUARY		IN BILLETS at ST. MAXENT	

J.M.
Major R.H.A.
Comdg. "N" Battery R.H.A.

SERIAL NO. 221

Confidential

War Diary

of

"N" Battery, Royal Horse Artillery.

FROM 1st February 1916 TO 29th February 1916.

WAR DIARY
INTELLIGENCE SUMMARY

Army Form C. 2118

Instructions regarding War Diaries and Intelligence Summaries are contained in F.S. Regs., Part II. and the Staff Manual respectively. Title Pages will be prepared in manuscript.

"N" BATTERY R.H.A. (I or S).

FEBRUARY 1916

Place	Date	Hour	Summary of Events and Information	Remarks and references to Appendices
ST MAXENT	FEB 1st-7th		In Billets at ST MAXENT.	
MARTAINNEVILLE	8th		Moved Billets to MARTAINNEVILLE.	
"	17th		In Billets at MARTAINNEVILLE.	
"	18th		Battery marched to GAMACHES and Entrained with "V" and "X" Batteries and Div: Ammn: Cm: Gun Section, to be attached to 1st ARMY	
VIEILLE CHAPELLE	19th		Battery Detrained at BETHUNE at midday and into Billets near VIEILLE CHAPELLE attached to 36th Division.	
	20th 21st		Reconnaissances of trenches round GIVENCHY carried out. Battery in Billets.	
	22nd		Two 18 PDR guns taken over from B/157 Battery, also 1 sub-section & 15 men attached for instructing. Their guns with our own Detachments under Lieut Fenton went into action after dark with 1st Line E. of our GIVENCHY. Range about 2200 yds to German trenches. Very severe weather, snow and frost.	
	23rd		Two more guns of B/157 R.H.A. with 1 subaltern, and 15 men taken over. Frost & snow.	
	24th		Wire cutting carried out with Right Section on a position of the German front trench line. 140 Rounds fired with good results. Two more guns under Lieut Hunt Grubbe with N/Battery's detachments and the 4th Artillery personnel attached, went into action after dark in dart position 1000 yds S. of 1st Section position. Range to German front line about the same. 1 W/Section fired 100 more rounds at their wire and 2nd Section 150 rounds at same with good effect.	Grubbe?
	25th		Capt Martin forward obs. from front trenches.	
	26th		1 w/Section Officer + Detachment relieved by Lieut Anthram and other Gunners.	
	27th		2nd Section fired 1415 on their wire, cutting 40 yds clean. Capt Martin worked with obs from front line trench. 1st Section moved back a few hundred yards to another position. 1 Section fired 12 rounds into LA BASSEE cherry night.	

1875 Wt. W593/826 1,000,000 4/15 J.B.C. & A. A.D.S.S./Forms/C. 2118.

WAR DIARY
INTELLIGENCE SUMMARY

(Erase heading not required.)

"N" BATTERY. R.H.A. FEBRUARY 1916 *(continued)*

Army Form C. 2118

Place	Date	Hour	Summary of Events and Information	Remarks and references to Appendices
	1916 28TH		Thiepval. Right Section a few Howitzer shells on their new position.	
	29TH		Neither section fired. Considerable activity of German Artillery.	

Gunmaster Capt
Comdg "N" Battery R.H.A.
for Major R.H.A.

SERIAL NO. 221.

Confidential

War Diary

of

"N" Battery, Royal Horse Artillery

FROM 1st March 1916 TO 31st March 1916.

Army Form C. 2118

WAR DIARY / INTELLIGENCE SUMMARY

(Erase heading not required.)

"N" BATTERY. R.H.A.   MARCH 1916

Place	Date	Hour	Summary of Events and Information	Remarks and references to Appendices
YTRES CHAPEL	MARCH 1st 2nd		Queedes Hay rather active front. Neither section fired.	
			Isolation Officer fired. Heavy firing just S. of us in the evening. Right section relieved by Centre section. Isolation Officer and 12 out of the 30 men of B.157 attached were transferred to another Battery to relieve congestion. 12 Gunners N.C.O.s R.H.A. sent to our Wagon line for a fortnight's instruction in Interior Economy of Horse mastership.	
	3rd		In Afternoon Left Section fired 162 rounds at wire with good effect. Capt. Offerton acted as forward Observing Officer from Trenches.	
	4th		Snowed all day. In Afternoon Right Section fired 25 rounds registering.	
	5th		In Afternoon Right Section twice again opened up on wire. Private PRUSSIAN was with success firing 102 rounds on to three rounds during the night. Reporting Enemy's working parties who were repairing at Right Section fired 154 rounds. Wire Cutting S. of SAXON WAY. In Afternoon very successful. Drew	
	6th		much retaliation on Chanvey Station	
	7th 8th		In morning all day Party of 3 Officers & 48 men from "I" Battery R.H.A. arrived to relieve us. Right Section fired 5 rounds and Left Section 3 rounds from etc. handed over to I Battery and detachments were much. Back to Wagon line.	
	9th		Battery marched to BETHUNE early and entrained. Detraining at DAOUR at LONGEAU and marching out immediately to billets at NAOURS 15 miles N.W.	
NAOURS	10th 15th		AMIENS and marching out immediately to billets at NAOURS In billets at NAOURS.	
	16th		Major R.H.D. Neat R.H.A. left for 20th Division. to take command of 93rd Bde. R.F.A.	
HAVERNAS	19th		Battery moved to HAVERNAS	
	22nd		Lieut C.G. Meiseggros R.F.A. attached for Duty	
	23rd 31st		Major F.N. French R.H.A. proceed from 1.7 Battery R.F.A. 2nd Division In billets " HAVERNAS	

T. French
Major, R.H.A.
Commanding "N" Battery, R.H.A.

SERIAL NO. 221.

Confidential

War Diary

of

"N" Battery, Royal Horse Artillery

FROM 1st May 1916 TO 31st May 1916.

WAR DIARY or INTELLIGENCE SUMMARY

Army Form C. 2118

Instructions regarding War Diaries and Intelligence Summaries are contained in F. S. Regs., Part II. and the Staff Manual respectively. Title Pages will be prepared in manuscript.

(Erase heading not required.) 31. V. 16

Place	Date	Hour	Summary of Events and Information	Remarks and references to Appendices
HAVERNAS	1st		In Billets	
	9th		Marched from HAVERNAS to DOMVAST	
	10th		for Divisional training	
	13th		In Billets + training	
	14th		Marched from DOMVAST to ACHEUX	
	15th		In Billets	
	16th		"	
	17th		"	
	18th		"	
	19th		"	
	20th		"	
	21st		"	
	22nd		→ Started 14 days Section training	
	23rd		"	
	24th		"	
	25th		"	
	26th		"	
	27th		"	
	28th		"	
	29th		"	
	30th		"	
	31st		"	

Capt., R.H.A.
Commanding "N" Battery, R.H.A.

SERIAL NO. 221.

Confidential
War Diary
of

"N" Battery, Royal Horse Artillery

FROM 1st June 1916 TO 30th June 1916.

WAR DIARY
or
INTELLIGENCE SUMMARY

(Erase heading not required.) **JUNE 1916**

Army Form C. 2118

Instructions regarding War Diaries and Intelligence Summaries are contained in F. S. Regs., Part II. and the Staff Manual respectively. Title Pages will be prepared in manuscript.

Place	Date	Hour	Summary of Events and Information	Remarks and references to Appendices
ACHEUX	1st		Marched to ALLENNAY.	
ALLENNAY	2nd		In Billets	
			To gun & mortar practice.	
			Returned to ACHEUX	
ACHEUX			In Billets	
ST RICQUER			Marched to ST. RICQUER for Divisional training	
			Divisional training	
RIENCOURT			Marched to RIENCOURT	
BUSSY-les-DAOURS	28th		Marched to BUSSY-les-DAOURS.	
			In Billets	
	30th		Bivouac	

Signed,
Major, R.H.A.
Commanding "N" Battery, R.H.A.

SERIAL NO. 221.

Confidential

War Diary

of

"N" Battery, Royal Horse Artillery

FROM 1st July 1916 TO 31st July 1916.

Army Form C. 2118

WAR DIARY or INTELLIGENCE SUMMARY

N Battery R.H.A.

JULY 1916

(Erase heading not required.)

Place	Date	Hour	Summary of Events and Information	Remarks and references to Appendices
BUSSY-LES-DAOURS	1ST	1.30AM	Marched with rest of Brigade to BURE SUR L'ANCRE, arrived 6.45AM. 1st day of BRITISH and FRENCH attack immediately No 5. of R. SOMME. Remained saddled up off the shelter material all day. Cavalry not required. Returned to bivouac at 6.30 P.M.	
ditto	2ND to 12TH		Bivouac. Officers made trips to reconnoitre crossings over river & captured time systems and lines of further advance.	
MEAULTE	13TH	8.0 AM	Moved to bivouac 1½ miles S.E. of MEAULTE arriving 2.30 P.M.	
	14TH		At 1.30 A.M. moved off with rest of Brigade to position of assembly N.E. of BRAY. Infantry attack at 3.25 A.M. At 6.30 A.M. moved on to near BRONFAY FARM & thence to valley S. of MONTAUBAN arriving there at 9.30 A.M. No opportunity for using Cavalry beyond pushing patrols until late in afternoon. At 5.40 P.M. 7TH. D. Gs, 6th, & 20TH. DECCAN HORSE attacking & Battery moved off 7TH. D. G's to cover right flank of 7TH. Division attacking FOUREAUX (or HIGH WOOD), & 20TH. to cover left flank of 7TH. Division & German Infantry about 700 yards S. of German DELVILLE WOOD. Battery moved into central position about 900 yards S. W. of LONGUEVAL to support the 2ND. line captured that day & about 900 yards Observation from German 2nd line support trench. Cavalry first went off at 8.10 P.M. 7TH. Division got to edge of HIGHWOOD without serious opposition. Only fired 21 rounds. 7TH. Division & Deccan Horse & Germans in ambush were running from relative positions of Deccan Horse & Germans from HIGH WOOD & DELVILLE WOOD not sufficiently clear in failing light to permit Battery firing. Between 11 P.M. & midnight 3 or 4 15cm. H.E. shell fell in Battery	

Army Form C. 2118

Continued

WAR DIARY
or
INTELLIGENCE SUMMARY N Battery R.H.A.

JULY 1916

(Erase heading not required.)

Instructions regarding War Diaries and Intelligence Summaries are contained in F.S. Regs., Part II. and the Staff Manual respectively. Title Pages will be prepared in manuscript.

Place	Date	Hour	Summary of Events and Information	Remarks and references to Appendices
	14TH		wagon line. Casualties: 2 men killed, 10 wounded; 12 horses killed & 17 wounded (evacuated). At 1 A.M. returned to Valley S. of Montauban, 7TH D.G's, & 20TH. Decca Horse forming up there too. At 7.30 A.M. returned to Bivouac.	
MEAULTE	15TH to 22ND		On Bivouac. During night 21ST—22ND. 2ND LT. MITCHELL took 2 teams out to bring in 2 captured 12 c.m. guns from N. edge of MAMETZ wood, but failed owing to one gun wheel being broken, & other gun overturned in a shell hole. Mules led back to camp bivouac that we left on 14TH, & remained there	
BUSSY-LES-DAOURS	23RD to 31ST.	6 P.M.	of month	

T. Friend
Major R.H.A.
Comdg. N Battery R.H.A.

Army Form C. 2118
5/100/1000

WAR DIARY   N Battery R.H.A.

INTELLIGENCE SUMMARY   August 1916.
(Erase heading not required.)

Place	Date	Hour	Summary of Events and Information	Remarks and references to Appendices
BUS-LES- ARTOIS	1st to 7th		Ordinary Routine. Tactical exercises for Officers + senior N.C.O.s 3rd, 4th, & 5th.	
ALLERY	8th	6.30am	Marched via AMIENS, PICQUIGNY, SOUES, ARRAINES, to ALLERY 26 miles. Billets	
TOEUFLES	9th	8am	Marches in OISEMONT to GUIMERVILLE (near SENARPONT) 14 miles. Bivouacs	
"	10th to 15th		Ordinary Routine.	
MOLLIENS-VIDAME	16th	7.30am	Marched via HORNOY, MOLLIENS-VIDAME to AILLY-SUR-SOMME 26 miles. Billets.	
FRICOURT	17th	8.0am	Marched via AMIENS, ST-GRATIEN to FRECHENCOURT 15 miles. Billets. C.O. & Battery leaders entrained of & FRICOURT & reconnoitred position for guns E. of BAZENTIN-LE-PETIT	
"	17th to 31st		Attached IIIrd Corps for use in forthcoming offensive.	

T. Fred
Major R.H.A.
Commanding N Battery R.H.A.

Army Form C. 2118

WAR DIARY N BATTERY R.H.A.

or INTELLIGENCE SUMMARY SEPTEMBER 1916

(Erase heading not required.)

Instructions regarding War Diaries and Intelligence Summaries are contained in F.S. Regs., Part II. and the Staff Manual respectively. Title Pages will be prepared in manuscript.

Place	Date	Hour	Summary of Events and Information	Remarks and references to Appendices
	1		Attached to III Bde. Corps for use in operations of reserve.	N/A
			Ypres Secondrated Cavalry Brigade.	799/1106
			Under the orders of O.C. Royal Canadian Horse Artillery
			Night patrols mainly E. of FRICOURT
			Relieved Ayrshire Secondrated Cavalry Brigade.
			Hd Quarters Carnivron Gds Artillery — near Whatcomb
			Attached to XV TH Corps for use in operations of reserve

T. Enoch
Major R.H.A.
Commanding N Battery R.H.A.

SERIAL NO. 22/.

Confidential
War Diary
of

"N" Battery, Royal Horse Artillery

FROM 1st October 1916 TO 31st October 1916.

OCTOBER 1916.

WAR DIARY

INTELLIGENCE SUMMARY

Vol IV

N BATTERY R.H.A.

Army Form C. 2118

Place	Date	Hour	Summary of Events and Information	Remarks and references to Appendices
BUSSY-LES-DAOURS	1st to 5th	–	In Bivouac. Attached to XVth Corps to be used when required.	
In Action	6th	9.30 pm	Moved into action at S.10 a 59 about 200 yards S. by E. of High Wood. Attached 21st Divisional Artillery.	
	7th		Covered an attack by 30th Division at 1.45 p.m. on line immediately S. of Eaucourt L'Abbaye — Le Barque Road. Attack failed.	
	11th		Line under R.H.A. group consisting of D, E, J, N, & X.	
	12th		Attack of 7th repeated at 2.5 p.m. Again failed.	
	15th & 16th		Took part by day & night in preliminary bombardment	
	18th		Attack of 7th repeated at 3.40 a.m. Raining wet. Again failed. Battery fires about 1000 rounds from 3.40 a.m. to 4.40 a.m.	
	25th & 26th		Prepared a position for one Section to go forward, just N. of Eaucourt L'Abbaye — Flers Road & about 1000 yards N.E. of Flers. Very exposed position, but not to be occupied yet.	
	27th		D, E, & J Batteries went out of action. We came under orders of 63rd. O/c R.F.A. 12th Division.	

PAGE 2. OCTOBER 1916. WAR DIARY N BATTERY R.H.A. Army Form C. 2118

INTELLIGENCE SUMMARY

GENERAL INFORMATION.

Weather throughout month very wet, rain almost every day. Frost 20th to 22nd. Weather largely responsible for failure of Infantry attack. Further attack due 25th. had to be postponed 3 times & not yet come off. Battery too far back, range 4400 to 5800. Position forward impossible to find, all forward slope. Battery fired about 8500 rounds 7th to 31st. Gun required constant watching; two main spring buffers just behind front flange on worn thin, had to be replaced. 4 sets of New springs, & 1 piston rod. Casualties Nil.

T. Freud
Major R.H.A.
Comdg. N Battery R.H.A.

WAR DIARY or INTELLIGENCE SUMMARY

N Battery R.H.A.
NOVEMBER 1916.

Army Form C. 2118.

Place	Date	Hour	Summary of Events and Information	Remarks and references to Appendices
In action o- SOMME. near H Gp W30	1st to 7th		On 5th event went trying for stack by 1ND. Australian Div. at 9:10 A.M. firing at slow rate nearly all day. Attached filled. Ammunition expended 1st to 7th, 1840 rounds.	G3A
	8th	5.30 A.M.	Moved guns out of action back to Wagon line.	
	9th	11 A.M.	Moved back. F. sub-sect near MEAULTE. Arrived of X Battery who had failed to get N sub out of action yet.	
ARGOEUVES	12th	6.45 A.M.	Marched via DAOURS, & AMIENS. Billeted	
METIGNY	13th	8.45 A.M.	Marched via PIQUIGNY, LES MESGES, & ARAINES. Billeted	
BEAUCHAMPS	14th	8.40 A.M.	Marched via OISEMONT & GAMACHES. Billeted, horses in open.	
	15th		Moved all horses under cover. Brig. Gen. SELIGMANN, C.R.A. Cavalry Corps inspected horses.	
	16th to 30th		Ordinary routine work. Horses, which had had very severe entitrain, Thinning work in hand, were much in need of rest. 3 drivers rejoined on 7th., 13 sent for details on 18th., & 23 received Quartet of Remounts on 23rd. but not inoculated at time out by order of D.A.D.V.S. Inoculated on 29th November middle.	

T. Grand
Major R.H.A.
Commanding N Battery R.H.A.

Army Form C. 2118.

INTELLIGENCE SUMMARY N Battery R.H.A.

Dec. 1916

Place	Date	Hour	Summary of Events and Information	Remarks references to Appendices
BEAUCHAMPS	1st		In rest billets. Ordinary routine work. One Officer (Lieut. Fenton) started annual leave. School for Junior Officers. Lt. Anderson attended Corps R.H.A. School for Junior Officers.	940 A99/365
	4th			
	31st			

Ormsby[?]

T. Snead[?]
Major R.H.A.
Commanding N Battery R.H.A.

BEF

2 IND. CAV. DIV.

Secunderabad Bde

Signal Troop

1914 Aug ᵗᵒ 1916 Dec

121/4046

W A R   D I A R Y

of Cavalry

Signal Troop Secunderabad Brigade

from 12th August to 30th November 1914.

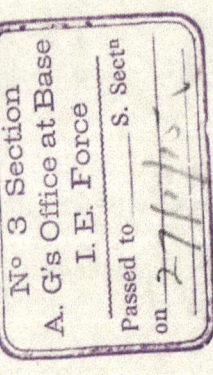

WAR DIARY
or
INTELLIGENCE SUMMARY

Army Form C. 2118

Hour, Date, Place	Summary of Events and Information	Remarks and references to Appendices
	Signal Troop 9th Secunderabad Cavalry Brigade	
August 12th - Bangalore -	Ordered by telegram to rejoin at Secunderabad and take over duties of Brigade Signalling Officer	
13th Secunderabad	Organization of Cavalry Brigade Signal Troop. This Troop did not exist as a unit in peace establishment & has to be improvised from units of the brigade for horses and personnel & its equipment from non-mobilized units of 1st Division. Personnel sanctioned — 1 Lieut. 1 Sergt. 6 R & 7 British 17 NCOs-men Indian (includes 6 despatch riders)	NB This improvisation from units of the brigade deprives them of signallers - Specially trained men have to replace —. The despatch riders from regt. are indifferently trained.
29th		
30th Secunderabad	12 Noon. Ordered by telegram to entrain for BOMBAY at 0.55 August 31st. Arrangements for conveyance of mens kits & equipment to station.	
31st "	Left Secunderabad at 0.55 AM	

Army Form C. 2118.

WAR DIARY
or
INTELLIGENCE SUMMARY
(Erase heading not required.)

Instructions regarding War Diaries and Intelligence Summaries are contained in F. S. Regs., Part II. and the Staff Manual respectively. Title pages will be prepared in manuscript.

2/

Hour, Date, Place	Summary of Events and Information	Remarks and references to Appendices
September 1st Bombay	Alexandria Dock 6am. Ordered to move into camp COOPERAGE till further orders. Orders same evening to be ready to embark on S.S. FULTALA.	
" 2nd "	Embarked S.S. FULTALA. Horses on board by ramp on to after upper deck where stalls were. No hitch. Moved into stream 5pm	
" 3rd Indian Ocean 9am	Ship rolling badly all the time. No chance of exercising horses on deck. Changed standings when possible. General loss of condition but not bad. Signalling communication of fleet by military Signallers - Flags - lamps	
" 10th Gulf of Aden	Calm - exercised horses.	
" 11th Aden	Horse D 116 taking fever Temp 106	
" 12th Red Sea	D 116 died midnight	
" 13th 14th 15th 16th Red Sea	Practised Signallers in reading Telephone buzzer	

Army Form C. 2118.

WAR DIARY
or
INTELLIGENCE SUMMARY

(Erase heading not required.)

Instructions regarding War Diaries and Intelligence Summaries are contained in F. S. Regs., Part II. and the Staff Manual respectively. Title pages will be prepared in manuscript.

3

Hour, Date, Place		Summary of Events and Information	Remarks and references to Appendices
September 17th	Suez	Arrived SUEZ 4pm entered canal 10pm.	
18th	Port Said	Arrived PORT SAID 10:30 am. Coaled	
19th to	Mediterranean	Fine weather nothing of note. Practice in Bunzen working.	
20th	"		
21st	"		
22nd	"		
26th	"		
27th	Marseilles	Arrived Marseilles. Anchored in outer Roads. Received disembarkation orders.	
27th	do.	Proceeded into harbour mole E arriving 2.30 pm. Disembarked. Exchanged rifles for new pattern. Moved to Camp LA PENNE arriving 9.30 p.m. Could not get Kit-up here so Camp so left there till next morning. Cold, heavy dew.	

WAR DIARY
or
INTELLIGENCE SUMMARY

(Erase heading not required.)

Army Form C. 2118.

Instructions regarding War Diaries and Intelligence Summaries are contained in F. S. Regs., Part II. and the Staff Manual respectively. Title pages will be prepared in manuscript.

4

Hour, Date, Place	Summary of Events and Information	Remarks and references to Appendices
Sep 29th Marseilles.	Camp LAPENNE. Replacing deficiencies, equipping troops from reinforce. dept. Conditioning horses. Weather fine. Any horses picked up quickly. Received orders to entrain morning of 5th	
30th "		
Oct 1st "		
2nd "		
3rd "		
4th "		
5th "	Left camp 6.30 arriving Gare de Breme 9.30. Entrainment complete 12.30.	
6th Rail.	Rail by ARLES, NIMES, CETTE, BEZIERES, TOULOUSE.	
7th Orleans.	Arrived Orleans 8pm. detrained moved into camp - LA SOURCE. Arrived 2am. Very cold.	

Army Form C. 2118.

WAR DIARY
or
INTELLIGENCE SUMMARY

(Erase heading not required.)

Instructions regarding War Diaries and Intelligence Summaries are contained in F. S. Regs., Part II. and the Staff Manual respectively. Title pages will be prepared in manuscript.

Hour, Date, Place	Summary of Events and Information	Remarks and references to Appendices
Oct 8th) ORLEANS 21st)	Camp - LA SOURCE. Despatch riding signalling schemes daily, map reading from French Ordnance map my indifferent equipment for motor cyclists.	
22nd	Secunderabad Cav.13th began to arrive	
23rd 24th 25th 26th 27th 28th	Camp LA. SOURCE.	
	Drew bicycles & two Kennel Telegraph from 7th D.G.S. me expedition from P.H	
29th	Entrained for the front	
30th	nil	
31st	Detrained at LILLERS marched ST VENANT where He concentrated; 3 motor cyclists joined	

Communications – 9th IND CAV BDE
1st NOV – 16th

FOSSE

- T LA CROIX MARMUSE
- Jodhpur Lancers JL
- T CAV FIELD Ambulance CFA
- Transport HQ
- N. RHA NRA **ZELOBES**
- Field Troop FT
- 7th Dragoon Guards DG
- HQ 9th IND CAV BDE *Vielle Chappelle*
- XX Deccan Horse DH
- Poona Horse PH amm Column HAL **LES LOBES**

MN ↑

--- --- = field telephone line
—dr— = despatch rider

WAR DIARY
or
INTELLIGENCE SUMMARY

(Erase heading not required.)

Army Form C. 2118.

Instructions regarding War Diaries and Intelligence Summaries are contained in F.S. Regs., Part II. and the Staff Manual respectively. Title pages will be prepared in manuscript.

Hour, Date, Place		Summary of Events and Information	Remarks and references to Appendices
Nov. 1st	VIEILLE CHAPELLE	Went into billets, having V. CHAPPELLE communication established with Indian Corps H.Qrs. and units of his Section. 1 Four telegraphist with a vibrator attached has loop from Intge Sig Coy to work corps line. Diagram of communications of bgs attached.	
Nov. 2nd	do.	VIEILLE CHAPELLE.	
8h.	do.		
9h.	6.30 p.m.	Marched to ESTAIRES. Troop billeted in factory E. of town. Bde acting as reserve to LAHORE Divn. Comn maintained by m/cyclist cyclist between Hartry Hqrs. Airnet.	
10h. 11h.	V. CHAPELLE	Nothing to note	
12h.		7th D.G's. moved to GORRE to replace a battalion in trenches. Communication between them via Indian Corps Machine divn Hqrs 2it by bde - by wire.	

Army Form C. 2118.

WAR DIARY
or
INTELLIGENCE SUMMARY

(Erase heading not required.)

Instructions regarding War Diaries and Intelligence Summaries are contained in F. S. Regs., Part II. and the Staff Manual respectively. Title pages will be prepared in manuscript.

Hour, Date, Place	Summary of Events and Information	Remarks and references to Appendices
November 13th Vieille Chapelle	Nothing to note. BOIRES. VIEILLE CHAPELLE. Communication as per diagram sheet 3	
14 hr		
15 hr		
16 hr		
do. 17 hr BETHUNE	Proceeded to new billeting area. Troop billeted in distillery SE of B in Bethune on Bethune Beuvry road. Telegraph section of 7th Sig Coy accompanied troop. Communication as per diagram attached.	
18 hr		
19 hr	Nothing to note.	
20 hr	7th Div moved to GONNEHEM. Communication with them by vibrator through corps hqs and enabled at 1800 q v 6 5. Thence by D1 cable laid by 7th Dyl GONNEHEM to ETHUEQUES. This worked very well thanks to assistance of corps sig coy in forwarding messages to Ethueques	

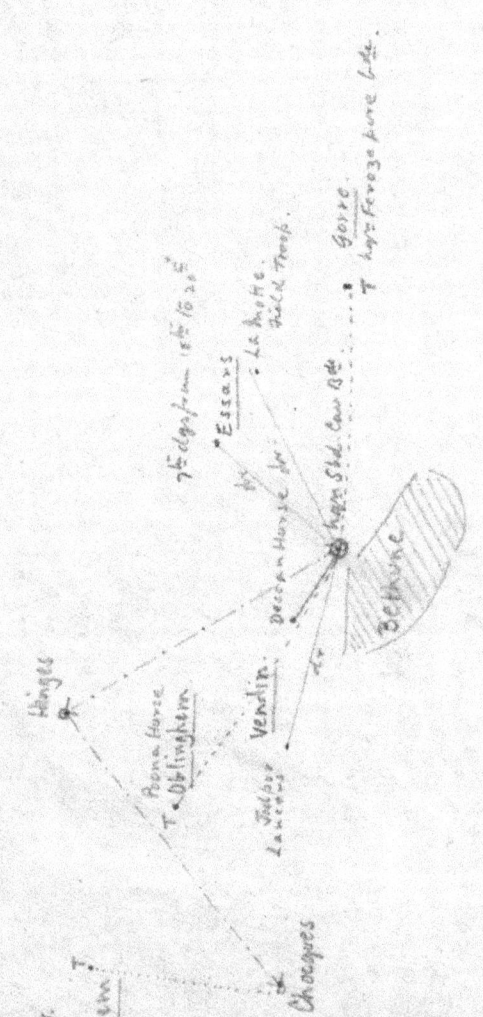

Army Form C. 2118

WAR DIARY
or
INTELLIGENCE SUMMARY
(Erase heading not required.)

Instructions regarding War Diaries and Intelligence Summaries are contained in F. S. Regs., Part II. and the Staff Manual respectively. Title pages will be prepared in manuscript.

Hour, Date, Place	Summary of Events and Information	Remarks and references to Appendices
November 21st BETHUNE 22nd	Nothing to note	
23rd	Detachment from the brigade proceeded to trenches at FESTUBERT attached to Ferozepore infantry brigade hqrs at JOERE. Established communication from detachment by using canal power line. Ist Gene with D1 instruments. Messages transmitted by S/Corp brigade see diagram page 7	
24th 30th	Nothing to note	

W R Kempson Lieut
Army Signal Troop
1/Indian Cav Bde

WAR DIARY

of

Signal Troop Secandrabad Cavalry Brigade.

From 1st November 1914 To 31st January 1915

Army Form C. 2118.

WAR DIARY
or
INTELLIGENCE SUMMARY

(Erase heading not required.)

Hour, Date, Place	Summary of Events and Information	Remarks and references to Appendices
1st December 1914 Bethune	Nothing to note.	
2nd	} nothing to note	
3rd	}	
4th	Relief by infantry of the detachment in the trenches. Out c/o the communication to gone.	
5th	No change	
6th	The brigade moved to the area BUSNES - DOUVE CREME (5 inch S. of ROBECQ) - CHOCQUES - BAS-RIEUX. Communications as per attached diagram	
7th/8th/9th	No change	

Stamp: ADJUTANT GENERAL INDIA W.D. 1877 - 7 FEB. 1915 BASE OFFICE

Stamp: No. 3 Section A. G's Office at Base I.E. Force Passed to S. Sectn Intelligence 7-2-15 S. Sectn Part II

WAR DIARY
INTELLIGENCE SUMMARY

(Erase heading not required.)

Army Form C. 2118.

Hour, Date, Place	Summary of Events and Information	Remarks and references to Appendices
December 11th 1914 Chateau Beaulieu - BUSNES		
12th	No change	
13th	do	
14th	do	
15th	do	
	Orders recd from Indian Corps for brigade to be ready from 5am on 16th to be used mounted or dismounted in aid of LAHORE DIVN	
16th 9am	Brigade assembled south of the O in LANNOY	
10am	Returned to billeting area	
17th	No change	
18th	Brigade warned to hold itself in constant readiness.	

Army Form C. 2118.

WAR DIARY
or
INTELLIGENCE SUMMARY
(Erase heading not required.)

Instructions regarding War Diaries and Intelligence Summaries are contained in F. S. Regs., Part II. and the Staff Manual respectively. Title pages will be prepared in manuscript.

Hour, Date, Place	Summary of Events and Information	Remarks and references to Appendices
December 19th 1914 BUSNES	Orders received from Indian Corps to send a dismounted detachment, strong as possible, to ANNEZIN to remain there in constant readiness. Detachment of 750 men under Lt. Dempsie proceeded as above. Signal Troop remained in billets, communications of billeting area maintained.	
" 20th	At 2.30 p.m. orders received for Bgd. to proceed to great to continue detachment. Bgde signed up into two motor cyclists proceeded by motor cycle. Got orders & 1 NCO & Telephone operators to follow mounted as quickly as possible. Brigade Headquarters was established in a house in RUE DE BETHUNE and Telephone communication was established to Headquarters BMERLEY Brigade and forward to the intermediate line of Trenches which were reoccupied by the brigade till 12:20 AM 21st.	

Army Form C. 2118.

WAR DIARY
or
INTELLIGENCE SUMMARY
(Erase heading not required.)

Instructions regarding War Diaries and Intelligence Summaries are contained in F.S. Regs., Part II. and the Staff Manual respectively. Title pages will be prepared in manuscript.

Hour, Date, Place	Summary of Events and Information	Remarks and references to Appendices
December 21st 1914 Rue de Bethune	At 12.20 am the bogate detachment moved up to FESTUBERT to take part in a counter attack. Communication by orderlies (on cycles) and telephone via Bareilly. Got up to right section FESTUBERT, also back to billeting area via Bareilly enjoint.	
22nd	Detachment came under orders of O.C. night section FESTUBERT. Communication by telephone & motorcyclist (road far better very bad & under water & commanded by enemy's snipers).	
7pm	Orders received for detachment to be withdrawn to a new billeting area, to come under Indian Cavalry Corps.	

Army Form C. 2118.

WAR DIARY
or
INTELLIGENCE SUMMARY

(Erase heading not required.)

13

Hour, Date, Place	Summary of Events and Information	Remarks and references to Appendices
December 23rd 1914	Detachment transported by motor lorries to new billeting area ISBERGUES - RELY - ESTREE BLANCHE.	
24 Th	Communications of brigade in new billeting area as per attached diagram	
25 Th	No change	
26 Th	No change	
27 Th	No change	
28 Th	No change	

Communications of
Secunderabad Cavalry Brigade
22.12.14

Field Telephone lines From Hqrs 2nd Indian cavalry division
via Hqrs Indian cavalry Corps.

To 7th DGS, DECCAN HORSE, POONA HORSE,
one instrument working 3 stations.

EME with all units by MOTOR CYCLIST
CYCLIST } despatch
MTD ORDERLIES } riders

HAMETZ
T
Hqrs 2nd INDIAN
CAV. DIVN

Hqrs. 2nd Cav Corps
T 3me St ANDRÉ

A.R.E.
Radinghem
MT. Cokunn
DR

"N" Battery RHA
LA RUPPE
DR
Bay field ambce
DR

Brigade
Headquarters
ISBERGUES
Bay field ambce

Le HAMEL
Manin Col
DR

Poona Horse
CAMBRES
DR
T 7th Dgs.
MOLINGHEM

Field Troop RE
BASSE RUE

Transport
Post Office
Supplies
Cord sance
T 30th Deccan Horse
LILETTE
MAZINGHEM

T = Field Telephone
----- = cable (not permanent)
——— = despatch riders

W. Campbell-Kent
Cmdg Signal Troop
Secbad Cav Bde

Army Form C. 2118.

WAR DIARY
or
INTELLIGENCE SUMMARY

(Erase heading not required.)

Instructions regarding War Diaries and Intelligence Summaries are contained in F. S. Regs., Part II. and the Staff Manual respectively. Title pages will be prepared in manuscript.

Hour, Date, Place	Summary of Events and Information	Remarks and references to Appendices
December 29th 1914 ISBERGUES	No change	
30th	No change	
31st	No change	W Blamphin Lieut Army Signal Troop Accountant Cav Bde

Serial No 247.

121/5799

WAR DIARY
OF

Signal Troop, Secunderabad Cavalry Brigade.

From 1st January 1915 To 31st May 1915.

Army Form C. 2118.

WAR DIARY
or
INTELLIGENCE SUMMARY

(Erase heading not required.)

Instructions regarding War Diaries and Intelligence Summaries are contained in F.S. Regs., Part II. and the Staff Manual respectively. Title pages will be prepared in manuscript.

[Stamp: A.G. OFFICE AT THE BASE — 13 JUN 1915 — INDIAN SECTION]

Hour, Date, Place	Summary of Events and Information	Remarks and references to Appendices
Estaires – 1st January 1915 to	During this month the brigade arrived in the billeting area Estaires – Molinghem – Lambres, Mazinghem, la Rompie. Communication as before by Telephone and despatch riders. Telephone operators got good practice working with existing telegraphs on the line from the landry hops hqrs. Three men detailed for duty on their instrument soon became proficient with vibrator reading & sending. Native telephone operators detached to instruct regimental signallers in working a line. Telegraphist method of reading without answering each word adopted. Regt. signallers soon became proficient in their method which is far quicker.	
11th Jan.	Brigade inspected by G.O.C. 2nd Ind. Car. Divn.	
18th Jan.	Concentration of Indian Car. Corps ½ mile W.N. Croix Inspection by Sir John French.	

Army Form C. 2118.

WAR DIARY
or
INTELLIGENCE SUMMARY

(Erase heading not required.)

Instructions regarding War Diaries and Intelligence Summaries are contained in F. S. Regs., Part II. and the Staff Manual respectively. Title pages will be prepared in manuscript.

Hour, Date, Place	Summary of Events and Information	Remarks and references to Appendices
ISBERGUES.		
Jan'y 28th 1915.	Brigade inspected by Genl. Rimington commanding Indian Cav: Corps.	
Jan'y 29th.	Orders received for brigade to be ready to move at 2 hrs notice communicated to Regts.	
February. 1st to 25th	Month of February spent in some area & training carried out. Despatch riding, flag & lamp schemes & Telephone work with regiments.	
	"N" battery left the brigade and proceeded to MERVILLE.	
March 1915. 3rd		
10—	Orders received for brigade to be ready to move at 1 hrs notice. Ruled in telephone lines to units communication by DR.	
10.36 pm	Brigade moved to move to position of readiness in the LE MAREQUET WOOD E. of ALLOUAGNE.	

1247 W 3299 250,000 (E) 8/14 J.B.C. & A. Forms/C. 2118/11.

Army Form C. 2118.

WAR DIARY
or
INTELLIGENCE SUMMARY

(Erase heading not required.)

Instructions regarding War Diaries and Intelligence Summaries are contained in F. S. Regs., Part II. and the Staff Manual respectively. Title pages will be prepared in manuscript.

Hour, Date, Place	Summary of Events and Information	Remarks and references to Appendices
March 11th 1915 ALLOUAGNE	Brigade remained in LE MAMETZ WOOD during day. Communication from HQ Divn to Bde by flag & light wire (telephone). Thence to Bdqrs. Divn etc by motor-cyclist & cyclist. Ordered into billets in evening.	
12th	Brigade in close billets. ALLOUAGNE. Wire laid from Divnn. one to units of Bde by cyclist & motor cyclist.	
13th	No change.	
14th	Brigade ordered to move back to old billeting area. If 2nd Army Corps.	
7.15 pm	Brigade moved out of ALLOUAGNE to THERDUANNE.	
15th March 1 am	Arrived new area MAMETZ – THERDUANNE – ENQUINEGATTE – BLESSY. Diagram of communications attached.	

Diagram of Communications
in the area THEROUANNE – MARTHES – MAMETZ.

Army Form C. 2118.

WAR DIARY
or
INTELLIGENCE SUMMARY
(Erase heading not required.)

Instructions regarding War Diaries and Intelligence Summaries are contained in F. S. Regs., Part II. and the Staff Manual respectively. Title pages will be prepared in manuscript.

Hour, Date, Place	Summary of Events and Information	Remarks and references to Appendices
March 1915. MAMETZ 16th —	No change	
17th —	Deccan Horse moved from ENGUINEGATTE to CRECQUES & MAMETZ. Nine MMTHES - ENGUINEGATTE relief in	
18th —	No change, nothing to report.	
31st —	No change	
April. 1st —	"N" Battery rejoined brigade & moved into billets at NIELLES — line laid from THEROUANNE - NIELLES.	
2nd —		
3rd — Th.	Bde moved into billets - ENGUINATTE with one squadron in REBECQ in order to vacate THEROUANNE for French Troops arriving N- S -	

Army Form C. 2118.

WAR DIARY
or
INTELLIGENCE SUMMARY

(Erase heading not required.)

Hour, Date, Place	Summary of Events and Information	Remarks and references to Appendices
Manel 5. April 6th	N battery vacated NIELLES & moved into billet RESER had line MARTHES - ENGUINEGATTE, & joined up Reser & unit to Div: line.	
12th	7th D.g.s and "N" battery returned to THEROUANNE & MELLES. Went old lines which had not been relieved up	
13th	7th D.g.s. and "N" battery march again to ENGUINEGATTE & NIESELD line in temporarily took Reserve of the Div line	
14th	Brigade moving up daily in lines to dig defensive line in neighbourhood of ST. VENANT.	
16th	7th D.g.s. moved from ENGUINEGATTE and RESER to billets PECQUEUR, HUCLECROM, LA RUVIE, and LE HAMEL.	

Army Form C. 2118.

WAR DIARY
or
INTELLIGENCE SUMMARY

(Erase heading not required.)

Instructions regarding War Diaries and Intelligence Summaries are contained in F. S. Regs., Part II. and the Staff Manual respectively. Title pages will be prepared in manuscript.

Hour, Date, Place	Summary of Events and Information	Remarks and references to Appendices
Mametz. April 24th 11.0am	Orders received for brigade to be ready to move at 2 hours notice. Communicated to units by motor cyclist.	
3.25pm	Brigade moved to turn out at once. Telephone lines MAMETZ – MARTHES, MAMETZ – CREEQUES cut up but 12 miles D1 cable and 4 miles light armoured wire into fighting troops & "A" echelon.	
4.25pm	Order received that 2nd Ind Cav Divn to move in support of 2nd Army.	
10 pm	Brigade arrived in new billeting area NOORDGENE – ZUYTPEENE – STUYVER. Signal troop in Chateau NOORDGENE. Communications by cyclist – miles cyclist from Divn HQ and to units.	
25th April	Informed that brigade would probably move during day.	
12.15 p.m.	Ordered to move at once. "B" echelon to remain behind. M wire telephone + lamp equipment in "A" echelon.	

Army Form C. 2118.

WAR DIARY
or
INTELLIGENCE SUMMARY
(Erase heading not required.)

Instructions regarding War Diaries and Intelligence Summaries are contained in F. S. Regs., Part II. and the Staff Manual respectively. Title pages will be prepared in manuscript.

Hour, Date, Place	Summary of Events and Information	Remarks and references to Appendices
28th April 6.30 pm 1 mile SW of PROVEN.	Reached billeting area at 6.30 pm 1 mile SW of PROVEN. Brigade in close billets. Communication by cyclist & motor cyclist & mounted orderly.	
29th April	Wire laid from Division by Signal Squadron.	
30th April	No change.	
1st May 11.15 pm	Orders received to move to billeting area in NOORDPEENE. Communicated by the usual personally in hole motor.	
2nd May 10.45 am	Brigade arrived in NOORDPEENE area	
3rd May	"N" Battery proceeded to join 1st Army	

Army Form C. 2118.

WAR DIARY
or
INTELLIGENCE SUMMARY
(Erase heading not required.)

Instructions regarding War Diaries and Intelligence Summaries are contained in F. S. Regs., Part II. and the Staff Manual respectively. Title pages will be prepared in manuscript.

Hour, Date, Place	Summary of Events and Information	Remarks and references to Appendices
4th May	Orders received for Bde to march back to old area billeting in BOMY - CUHEM - LAIRES - ERNY ST JULIEN Order communicated by motor cyclist. NB Captain to POONA HORSE home down + incident of morning meaning with man of 75 Regt in whose area he was to envoy men. In trial to meet machine emergence won Poona Horse received news note. Important in all men to Troop the serious consequences that might occur by mistakes of this kind	
5th May 5.00am	Brigade arrived in billeting area. Signal water in Château BOMY.	
6th May	Took over old lines left by Sialcote Brigade + worked them down to width	Diagram attached

Diagram of Communications
area BOMY–CUHEM–LAIRES.

ST.QUENTIN
● YCO

FONTAINE-LEZ-
HERMANS
● PIE

Test office on line
VIA - YCO
VIA - PIG
VIA - PIE

CUHEM
● CD
T
FLECHIN
●

Bomy
● BL+TT DR
T
DR
LAIRES
● BO

VIB
● K-
WANDONNE

23

Army Form C. 2118.

WAR DIARY
or
INTELLIGENCE SUMMARY
(Erase heading not required.)

Instructions regarding War Diaries and Intelligence Summaries are contained in F. S. Regs., Part II. and the Staff Manual respectively. Title pages will be prepared in manuscript.

Hour, Date, Place	Summary of Events and Information	Remarks and references to Appendices
May 7th BOMY	Orders from Sigs Oni tspn that in future in which no lines to be laid to regimental HQ & the nature to be used in Companies. Lines from Divn also working with Cnrs Hqs & other two brigades of Divn. Blocks in line frequent and upkeep of line difficult owing to its abnormal length. Good work by 3 operators forming Hq section. Enemy prevented delay to Em brigade. Power lines inoperative to portion of line passing through their area & M.O.s like portion frequent breakdowns of M.O.s like leading of line owing to length of line leading to current. No damage	

Army Form C. 2118.

WAR DIARY
or
INTELLIGENCE SUMMARY

(Erase heading not required.)

Hour, Date, Place	Summary of Events and Information	Remarks and references to Appendices
May 10th – 16th BOMY	No change.	
May 17th 2.10pm	Orders received & communicated by motor cyclist to unit - to be to turn out and move to FERFAY	
6.30pm	Orders for march & billeting received at AUCHEL communicated by motor orderlies along the column	
8.15pm.	Brigade reached clive billets in LAPUGNOY.	
May 18th	No change	
19th 1.35pm	Orders received for brigade to be ready to march to last billeting area by Divn at 2.30pm. To save time orders communicated verbally by tele Sig opr.	

2.5

Army Form C. 2118.

WAR DIARY
or
INTELLIGENCE SUMMARY

(Erase heading not required.)

Instructions regarding War Diaries and Intelligence Summaries are contained in F. S. Regs., Part II. and the Staff Manual respectively. Title pages will be prepared in manuscript.

Hour, Date, Place	Summary of Events and Information	Remarks and references to Appendices
May 1915		
6.15 pm	Brigade reached new billeting area as per attached diagram. Communications as per diagram.	
20th —		
31st —	No change	

W. Lamphrey
OC. Signal Troop

12/7286

WAR DIARY
with Appendices.

OF

Signal Troop, Secunderabad Cavalry Brigade.

From 1st August 1915 TO 30th September 1915.

WAR DIARY
or
INTELLIGENCE SUMMARY

(Erase heading not required.)

Army Form C. 2118.

Hour, Date, Place	Summary of Events and Information	Remarks and references to Appendices
August 1st 1915	Brigade marched from WANDONNE – FRUGES area to BRIMIEUX + in billets BRIMIEUX { hd Sqdrn, Signal Sqdrn, Signal Troop. MARTENLA – N. Butts AIX-EN-ISSART – 7 Bg BRUNHAUTPRÉ – Ponnaitomi BRIMIEUX – Decaunhom Communications to units in the anuich + in above area by motor cycling + cyclists. Communication by m. cyclist maintained with DIVL HQ which moved by a parallel route.	ARRAS sheet 7 1/80,000
6 p.m.	Orders to march in 2nd ½ to area junc. of ABBEVILLE Communication + units by m. cyclist.	
2nd Aug	Marched to area SIRIQUIER – ABBEVILLE – Château L'ABBAYE. Communications maintained as before.	

Army Form C. 2118.

WAR DIARY
or
INTELLIGENCE SUMMARY
(Erase heading not required.)

Instructions regarding War Diaries and Intelligence Summaries are contained in F. S. Regs., Part II. and the Staff Manual respectively. Title pages will be prepared in manuscript.

Hour, Date, Place	Summary of Events and Information	Remarks and references to Appendices
August 3rd	Marched to area CROUY - ST PIERRE - A - GOUY - SOUES	
August 4th 5th 6th 7th	Remained in above area	
8th	H.Q. and signal Troop marched to CHATEAU at CAVILLON. Orders received for a ro riper of Seabais side to move in 10ts to hold line of Trenches in neighbourhood of AUTHUILLE (known in Factor	

WAR DIARY or INTELLIGENCE SUMMARY

Army Form C. 2118.

Hour, Date, Place	Summary of Events and Information	Remarks and references to Appendices
10th August. —	Lieut Watson appointed to command of F sector with him own staff - reorganization of Signal Troop to meet requirement of (F) Lieut Watson as sector commander. Col Elamie in commanding detachment of 9/10 Hpn in Sweeter Fe, working of lines in permanent billets. To do this it was necessary to bring two British operators with him on D3 Telephone from Corps Signals. Put sufft Ellis in command of section to run Col Elamies communications, taking over communication of F sector myself. See attached diagram.	
7.15 am	9/10 super with signal troop embarked at ST. PIERRE A - GOUY to FRANVILLERS	
11h 15	Party halted at FRANVILLERS	
12h 9pm	Party left FRANVILLERS for MARTINSART	

Diagram shewing system of communications employed in trenches of sector (F) commanded by Genl. Wadeson. The diagram is not to scale. It is to indicate how the existing infantry lines were used to meet requirements of the cavalry detachment.

– – – – – – – Lines operated & maintained by the sector sigl oft.
– ·· – ·· – ·· Lines operated & maintained by the sub-sector sigl ofrs.
–·–·–·–·– Lines operated & maintained by regimental signallers

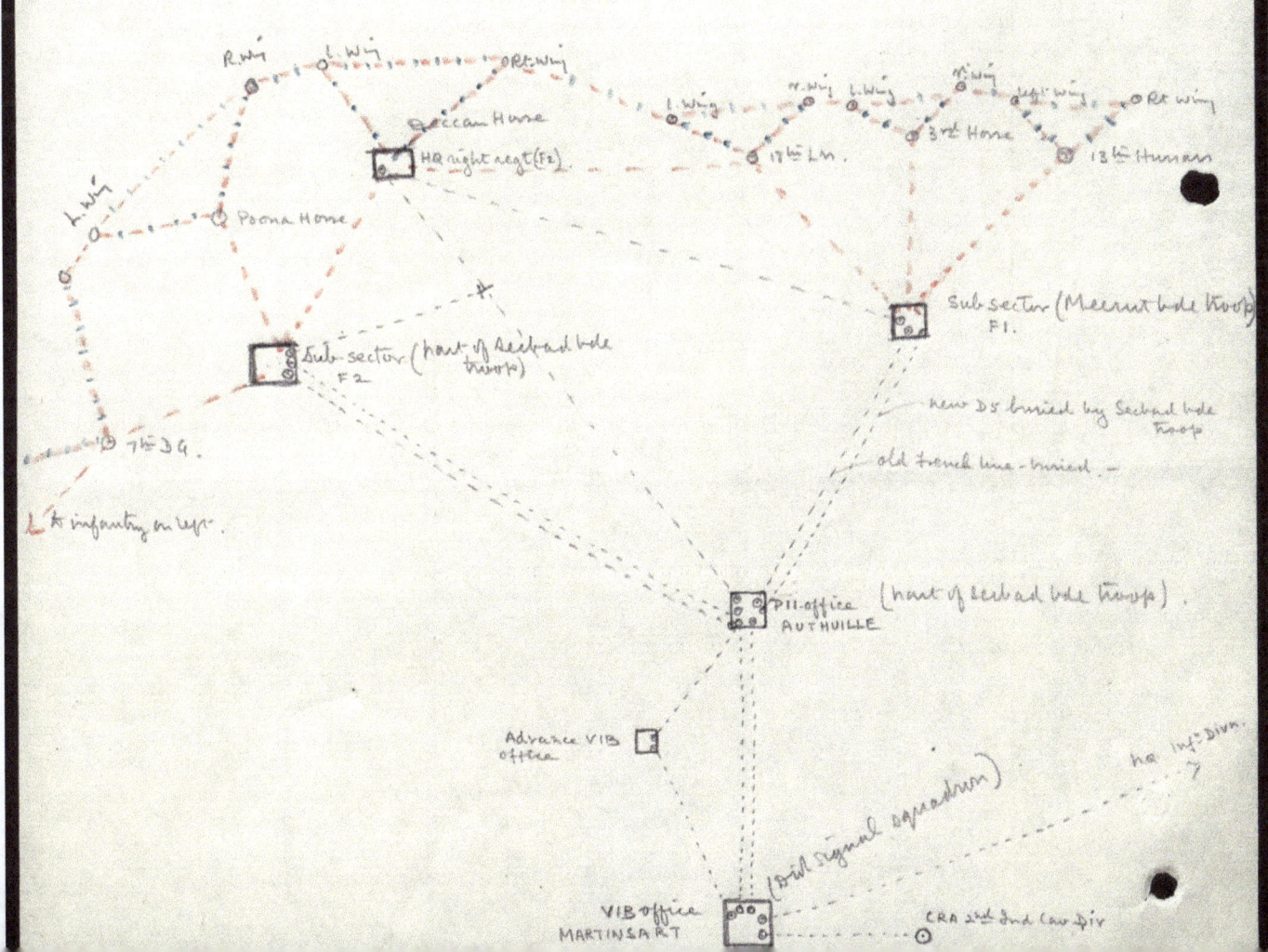

WAR DIARY
or
INTELLIGENCE SUMMARY
(Erase heading not required.)

Army Form C. 2118.

Hour, Date, Place	Summary of Events and Information	Remarks and references to Appendices
August 13th	Relief of 152nd Infantry Brigade by 2nd Ind. East Div. Took over Signal office of reserve battn at AUTHUILLE as my sector signal office. Despatched Sergt Ellis with his detachment of the troop to take over signal office of the <s>centre</s> left battalion as signal office of D.T.C. left subsector (Fr). Regiment Stuart Capt Henry with meant the troop taking over Right subsector office as right subsector (Fr) office it coming under my orders. By 11pm. communication was established from sector office through to all advanced telephone dug outs in front trenches.	
14th Aug 1 am.	Relief complete — communication nr front as two many telephones all working together on same lines defending each other's work. Reorganisation of whole system appeared necessary.	

Army Form C. 2118.

WAR DIARY
or
INTELLIGENCE SUMMARY
(Erase heading not required.)

Instructions regarding War Diaries and Intelligence Summaries are contained in F. S. Regs., Part II. and the Staff Manual respectively. Title pages will be prepared in manuscript.

Hour, Date, Place	Summary of Events and Information	Remarks and references to Appendices
15th	Rearranging existing communications to suit requirements of the cavalry detachment. Tracing lines reconnecting lines + readjusting switch boards in accordance telephone dug-out. Excellent work by Sergt Skirt in this matter	
16th – 21st	Reorganisation completed. — Communication main interrupted + all signalers in front + regiment worked excellently well. Buried a new line to F1 sub-sector.	
21st –	Orders to relieve by 1st and 2nd Cav Div.	
22nd – 5pm	Relief commenced. (Served by Sidewire)	
23rd – 5pm	Relief continued	
24th – 3am	Relief completed.	

WAR DIARY
or
INTELLIGENCE SUMMARY

(Erase heading not required.)

Army Form C.-2118.

Instructions regarding War Diaries and Intelligence Summaries are contained in F. S. Regs., Part II. and the Staff Manual respectively. Title pages will be prepared in manuscript.

Hour, Date, Place	Summary of Events and Information	Remarks and references to Appendices
August 24th - 31st	The trench party employed digging second line trenches under Col. Blamie. Placed one motor-cyclist (Pte. HAWKINS) and three cyclists at the disposal of this party for inter-communications. Pte Hawkins did excellent work as motor-cyclist. Having been thoroughly instructed by Cpl Peterson he is now a perfectly reliable man in any situation with a motor-cycle.	

WAR DIARY
or
INTELLIGENCE SUMMARY

(Erase heading not required.)

Army Form C. 2118.

Instructions regarding War Diaries and Intelligence Summaries are contained in F. S. Regs., Part II. and the Staff Manual respectively. Title pages will be prepared in manuscript.

Hour, Date, Place	Summary of Events and Information	Remarks and references to Appendices
September 1st. 1915	Signal troops moved up in evening from CAVILLON to join the advanced Tenth party under Col Rennie, leaving three motor cyclist and two telephone operators to work the communications between CAVILLON and the hqrs of the Division.	
2nd	In the night of the second Col Rennie's party of 90 after relieved the Durham Brigade & became the supporting brigade of the sector in AUTHVILLE village. The signal troop took over the communications of AUTHVILLE defences (see map attached) and assisted Capt Henry to work the communications *communications of the sector. The sector	
3rd	AUTHVILLE. Communication work normal between the trenches & the sector signal office. driven up the	
12th	Village, defences tested & hastened daily by Sig troops.	

WAR DIARY
or
INTELLIGENCE SUMMARY

(Erase heading not required.)

Army Form C. 2118.

Hour, Date, Place	Summary of Events and Information	Remarks and references to Appendices
Night of 12th – 13th	The detachment of the Squadron and Brigade was relieved by the Divisional Brigade, the communications being taken over by that brigade signalling off'r.	
September 13th	Col Blair's detachment marched to ST GRATIEN where today 300 men remained to dig second line. One motor cyclist and two cyclists attached to this party. Remainder of troop returned to CAVILLON.	
September 15th to September 22nd	CAVILLON. – Continued training of despatch riders and visual signallers. Orders received for brigade to march to billet in FIENVILLERS – VACQUERIE, GORGES, DOMESNIL, EPECAMPS. Owing to departure of Cpl. A and R. Patman to England to train for commissions had to borrow a motor cyclist from the Divl. Signal Squadron for the purpose of keeping up their wire.	

WAR DIARY
or
INTELLIGENCE SUMMARY

(Erase heading not required.)

Army Form C. 2118.

Hour, Date, Place	Summary of Events and Information	Remarks and references to Appendices
September 22nd 7pm	Arrived FIENVILLERS. Headquarters, Decean House — Personnel Horses — billeted in that village. 7th Bgd. in VACQUERIE, EPECAMPS, DOMESMONT. N battery in GORGES. Communication by motor cyclist and cyclist.	
23rd	FIENVILLERS —	
24th	Two motor-cyclists joined from from MOEVILLE (neither of them mechanics.)	
25th	FIENVILLERS. no change. No telephone communication with division — Roads very bad and have no motor-cycles.	
30th		

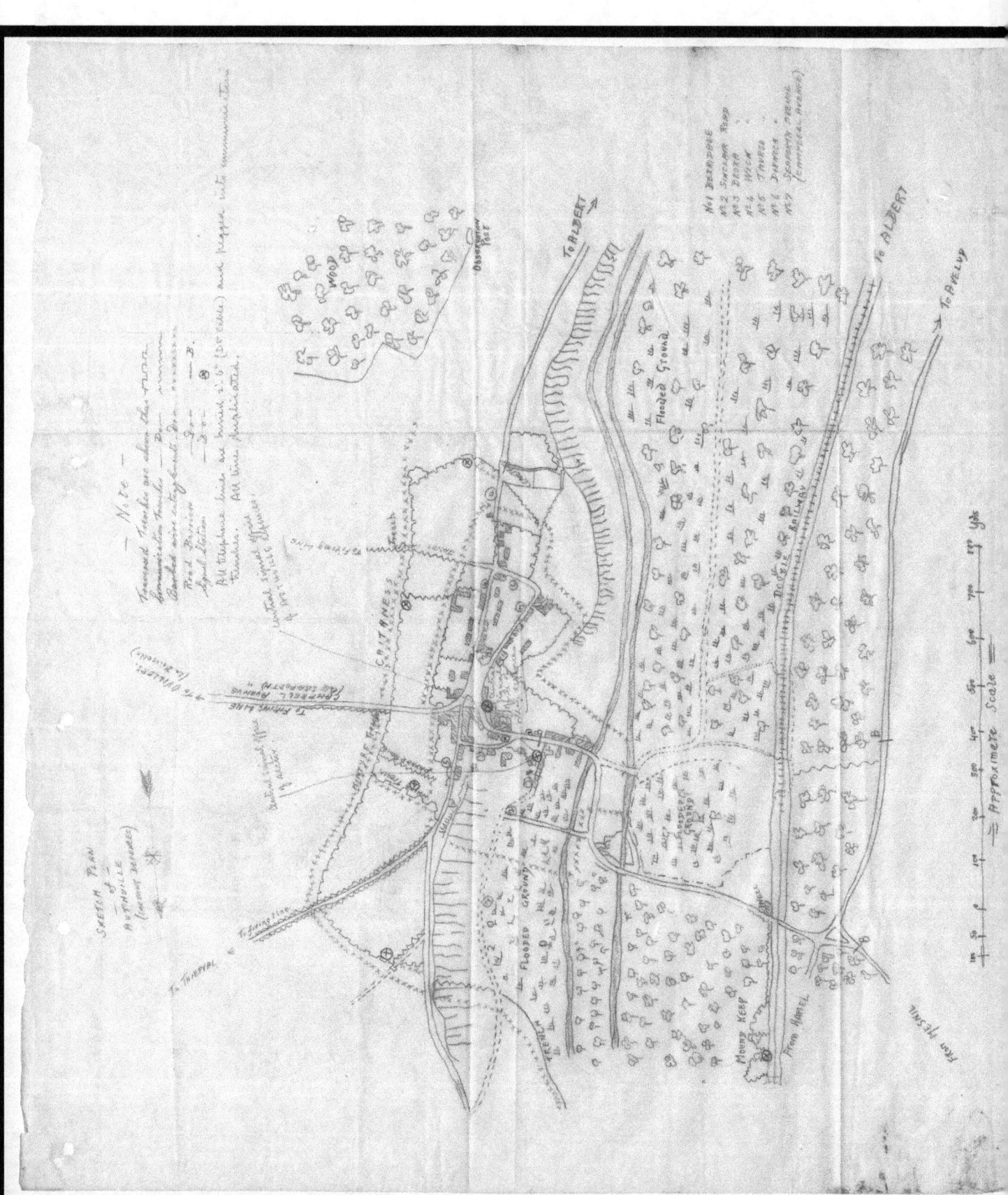

Serial No. 247.

Confidential
121/7601

War Diary
with appendices.
of

Secunderabad Cavalry Brigade Signal Troop

FROM 1st October 1915. TO 31st October 1915.

Army Form C. 2118.

WAR DIARY
or
INTELLIGENCE SUMMARY
(Erase heading not required.)

Instructions regarding War Diaries and Intelligence Summaries are contained in F. S. Regs., Part II. and the Staff Manual respectively. Title pages will be prepared in manuscript.

Hour, Date, Place	Summary of Events and Information	Remarks and references to Appendices
1st to 5th October FIENVILLERS	Nothing to report	
5th	Divisional scheme. Mrs. Difficulty of motorcyclists + cyclists keeping touch with horse when it moves across country. Mounted men must be kept in readiness to take in their messages.	
6th – 14th FIENVILLERS	Nothing to report. Carried out schemes daily for despatch riders moving across country in touch with cyclists moving by roads to notify moves of Sn.	
14th	Brigade moved to new billeting area RIBEAUCOURT – LONGVILLERS – DOMQUEUR – GORENFLOS. Signal Troop in RIBEAUCOURT. Communications made by despatch rider. Telephone communication to 1st Ind Cav Divn.	

WAR DIARY or INTELLIGENCE SUMMARY

Army Form C. 2118.

Hour, Date, Place	Summary of Events and Information	Remarks and references to Appendices
RIBEAUCOURT 14th – 22nd	Nothing to report – carried out daily scheme of inter-communication. On 19th a divisional scheme – dismounted attack on village. Communication to Divn and units by telephone. Field light enamelled wire laid by runners behind the attacking troops. Found it useless but at one of my communication mules – impossible to mend it. Substituted D1 which worked well. Intercommunication units rather slow into flag when telephone failed. In a dismounted attack units should drop posts of 2–3 men at intervals of 300x and manage traffic by runners using these posts as relays. This has been found by the infantry to be the best means of communication back to Bde HQrs.	
22nd	Brigade moved to area PONT-REMY – BAILLEUL – LIMEUX – DOUDLAINVILLE – ST MAXENT – CERISY – Signal troop in PONT REMY. Deccan Horse in LIERCOURT – FRONDELLE – BELLEFONTAINE	

WAR DIARY
or
INTELLIGENCE SUMMARY

Army Form C. 2118.

Hour, Date, Place	Summary of Events and Information	Remarks and references to Appendices
October 22nd PONT-REMY	– BAILLEUL. Pomme Hine in DOUDLAINVILLE – VAUX MARQUENVILLE, 7th D&S. in CERISY – FRESNE – TILLOLOY N Battery in ST MAXENT. Owing to this my attended men, state of roads + weather, established a relay post of 1 corporal 2 signallers 2 motorcyclist 6 men dn at POULTIERES which is materially equidistant and close to DOUDLAINVILLE – ST MAXENT CERISY. All communications to Pomme Hime – 75 Bays – N Battery to go + come +go via the relay post, attached units) orders etc with reference to the me of the relay post. (2) orders to the relay post (3) Diagram of the area. Applied for civic air line to establish Telephone comm with units.	DOUDLAINVILLE – VAUX MARQUENVILLE – FRESNE – TILLOLOY
U.R. 28th —1945	Printed civil signal spht to lay civic air line PONT–REMY – OISEMENT	

Army Form C. 2118.

WAR DIARY
or
INTELLIGENCE SUMMARY

(Erase heading not required.)

Instructions regarding War Diaries and Intelligence Summaries are contained in F. S. Regs., Part II. and the Staff Manual respectively. Title pages will be prepared in manuscript.

Hour, Date, Place	Summary of Events and Information	Remarks and references to Appendices

—·—·— = enemy air line (galvanised wire)
·········· = D¹ insulated cable
———— = DR
〰〰〰 = Regtl. lines D¹

(P11) = Sebastow Bde HQ
(RP) = Relay Post
(UN) = "N" RHA
(TT) = 7th Dgs.
(CCA) = Poona Horse
(YCG) = Ind Cav Corps
(VIB) = 2nd Ind Cav Div
(P1G) = [illegible]

Diagram of intercommunication
Oct 31st 1915.

M. Campbell Hope
Signals P11

To The Officers Commanding All Units,
    Secunderabad Cavalry Brigade.
CR 55.   23rd October 1915.
COMMUNICATIONS.

From Noon 24th inst a relay post found by Signal Troop will be established in POULTIERES (1 mile N of DOUDELAINVILLE).

1. All messages for 7th Dragoon Guards, "N" Battery and 34th Poona Horse, will be delivered at the relay post and transmitted from there.

2. All messages from the above units for Brigade Hd Qrs should be delivered at the relay post for transmission.

3. The orderlies of the above units, who at present report at 4 pm daily for Routine Orders at Bde Hqrs will in future report at the relay post at that hour.

4. The letters and parcels of the above units will be delivered by the Signal Troop to the relay post and taken on to units by the above 4 pm orderlies. (This is subject to time of arrival of post lorry at Bde Hqrs, any change will be notified).

5. The Relay post motor-cyclist will assist the O.C. Poona Horse with any Urgent communications to his outlying Squadrons.

6. The present area being difficult for communications, and in view of approaching bad weather and bad roads "Urgent" communications should be reduced to a minimum.

                                W.T.Campbell / Captain.
                            Signals Secunderabad Cavalry Brigade.

ORDERS FOR RELAY POST.

1. **DUTIES.** One British Rank to be on Duty in Office by day & night.

    He will be in charge of the abstract and will be responsible for transmission of all messages delivered at the post.

2. Messages marked "<u>Urgent</u>" or "<u>Priority</u>" and franked by an Officer authorised to do so, to be sent off at once by motor cyclist.

3. Should a Motor Cyclist from Brigade Hd Qrs arrive with an "Urgent" despatch and find the Relay Post Motor Cyclist out he should be sent on at once with the message (it should not be left in the office until the Relay post Motor Cyclist returns.

4. All matter not marked "Urgent" should be sent on by Cyclist and Mounted Despatch Riders.

5. **POSTS.** Matter not marked "Urgent" should be collected and sent out from the Relay Post at the following times:—

To <u>UNITS</u>	To Bde Hd Qrs
7 am	Forwarded by any
12 Noon	Motor Cyclist returning
4 pm (Regtl Orderlies)	to Bde Hd Qrs.

6. The Motor Cyclist at the post will be prepared to assist the O.C. Poona Horse for "<u>Urgent</u>" despatches to his outlying squadrons.

7. Mails for Regiments except D. Horse will be delivered at the Relay Post by 2 pm daily, and will be handed over to Regimental Orderlies at 4 pm, or earlier if units send for them.

8. All men on post must be in billets by 8.30 pm.

9. Telephone cue will be established from Bde HQ via Divn - 7th DGS, N Battery, Poona Horse & Relay Post as quickly as possible.

W. Campbell Captain.
"Signals" Secunderabad Cavalry Brigade.

SERIAL NO. 247.

Confidential

War Diary

of

Signal Troop, Secunderabad Cavalry Brigade.

FROM 1st November 1918 TO 31st January 1919.

Army Form C. 2118.

WAR DIARY
or
INTELLIGENCE SUMMARY
(Erase heading not required.)

Hour, Date, Place	Summary of Events and Information	Remarks and references to Appendices
Nov. 1 91- to 19 h	Billet PONT - REMY.	
7 h	Lt Nichull 1 Me joined Troop for training in duties as a signalling officer. To be attached for two minutes to Brigade troop - 1 month to Divisional squadron.	
19 h	Brigade Headquarters & signallers moved from PONT-REMY to TAUMONT. Relay post maintained at Hubby POULTIENES.	
	Revised diagram of intercommunication attached.	
19 h — 30 h	No change.	

CR/5.6
85/3/1/6
1/2

Army Form C. 2118.

WAR DIARY
or
INTELLIGENCE SUMMARY
(Erase heading not required.)

Instructions regarding War Diaries and Intelligence Summaries are contained in F. S. Regs., Part II. and the Staff Manual respectively. Title pages will be prepared in manuscript.

Hour, Date, Place	Summary of Events and Information	Remarks and references to Appendices

COMMUNICATIONS. SECUNDERABAD CAVALRY BRIGADE.
November 1915.

Ref.
— D.R.
~~~~~~ Comic Air Line.
·········· D.I. & D.S. Cable.

HEUCHENVILLE

○ LISACOURT.
H.Q. 2nd I.D. Horse.

○ SOREL.

○ HALLENCOURT.
I.C.C.

○ CAUMONT.
D.R.

Mob. Vet. Sec.
○ LINEUX.
34th P. Horse.

Relay Post.
○ POULTIERES.
D.R.
○ WARCHEVILLE.
34th P.G.M. 18th R.
○ DOUDELAINVILLE.
H.Q. 34 & 9 R. Horse.

○ FRESNE-Tilloloy.
9 R. Lys.

○ ST MARSBY.
H.B.Dy. 2a-Women.

○ CERISY.
H.Q. 7 & 9. G.G.

○ VILLEROMT.
H.Q. 2nd L.I. Car Divn.

N

Ref. Sheets 11 & 12. 80,000 Map.

Army Form C. 2118.

WAR DIARY
or
INTELLIGENCE SUMMARY

(Erase heading not required.)

Instructions regarding War Diaries and Intelligence Summaries are contained in F.S. Regs., Part II. and the Staff Manual respectively. Title pages will be prepared in manuscript.

Hour, Date, Place	Summary of Events and Information	Remarks and references to Appendices
December 1915 CAUMONT 1st – 15th	No change – Training at Nichets in office work – buzzer – line laying – repairing – visual signalling	
16th – 19th 11h15	Lt Nicholl jones with signal sqn moves from Dieu Decum true moved into area HUCHENVILLE – LIMERCOURT – HUPPY. Hqrs at LIMERCOURT. Squadron Formative moved from LIMEUX to GREBAULT-MESNIL. Diagram of communication lines attached. Mounted relay post from POULTIERES to HUPPY where they act as telephone station for supplies, post office & detachments of Decum true & deal with half to five visits in same manner as before. Cpl Moffitt in charge.	
16th – 31st	No change. Sigr VIB laid armoured line direct OISEMONT-CAUMONT with to visit up their cable St MAXENT-CAUMONT in HUCHENVILLE. Intended to 10 mile air line to replace this cable. Relay regimental line to attach by sqns. Proposed wire air line shown in Red in attached diagram.	

1217 W.2799 200,000 (E) 8/11 J.B.C. & A. Forms/C. 2118/11.

WAR DIARY
or
INTELLIGENCE SUMMARY

(Erase heading not required.)

Army Form C. 2118.

Hour, Date, Place	Summary of Events and Information	Remarks and references to Appendices
COMMUNICATIONS SECUNDERABAD CAVALRY BRIGADE DECEMBER 31st 1915.		PROPOSED NEW COMMUNICATION LINES

Ref:—
— · — · — D.R.
~~~~~~~ Civil Tel Line.
– – – – Div. D3 Cable.

Ref Sheet 11. 1/40,000 map.

Army Form C. 2118.

WAR DIARY
or
INTELLIGENCE SUMMARY

(Erase heading not required.)

Instructions regarding War Diaries and Intelligence Summaries are contained in F. S. Regs., Part II. and the Staff Manual respectively. Title pages will be prepared in manuscript.

Hour, Date, Place	Summary of Events and Information	Remarks and references to Appendices
January 1st – 31st 1916 CAUMONT	No change. Bde HQ remained in billets at CAUMONT. Proposed linen in the attached diagram were completed and insulated cable reeled in. Month chiefly occupied in training regimental signallers of Poona Horse, and Deccan Horse with a view to reclassification under new Signalling Regulations.	
	10.15. H.Q. Mahmud Jamn Khan was extremely useful instructing Deccan Horse in improving which has most important part of new test.	
29th, 30th & 31st	Held the classification test of the Deccan Horse Signallers. Result very satisfactory.	

W.Campbell Capt.
O.C. Signal Troop 7B de.
1.2.16

WAR DIARY
or
INTELLIGENCE SUMMARY

(Erase heading not required.)

Army Form C. 2118.

Hour, Date, Place	Summary of Events and Information	Remarks and references to Appendices
COMMUNICATIONS SECUNDERABAD CAVALRY BRIGADE. January 31st 1916. Ref:— ———— D.R. ———— To all Units. — · — · — Cable Airline. · · · · · · · · · D/3 — Broken Wire. Sheet H. 50,000 Map.	*[hand-drawn communications map showing locations: CAUMONT (7.H.) Bde Vet Sec, LIMEUCOURT HQ 20th D.H., GREBAULT MESNIL 2nd D.G., HUPPY R.T. Relay Stn., 20th Hus. Waggon Line Post Office Exchange, VAUDRICOURT 3rd 12 M.G., ST VINCENT M.D.R. R.H.A., BOUILLANCOURT HQ S.C. P. Wilson, FRESNE TILLOY 7th D.G., CERISY HQ 7 D.G., SENTE LINE, OISEMONT HQ 2nd I.V.D. — with north arrow]*	

W. Winfield Captain
Signals Sec.2nd Cav. Bde.

SERIAL NO. 247.

Confidential

War Diary

of

Signal Troop, Secunderabad Cavalry Brigade.

FROM 1st February 1916 TO 29th February 1916

Army Form C. 2118.

WAR DIARY
or
INTELLIGENCE SUMMARY

(Erase heading not required.)

Instructions regarding War Diaries and Intelligence Summaries are contained in F. S. Regs., Part II. and the Staff Manual respectively. Title pages will be prepared in manuscript.

Hour, Date, Place	Summary of Events and Information	Remarks and references to Appendices
February 1st 1916 – 3rd CAUMONT	No change – nothing to report.	
3rd	Brigade moved into new billeting areas as follows :- Bde HQ Signal Troops } ERCOURT 7th Dgs. CERISY – ST. MAXENT – MARTAINNEVILLE. N. Batt. ST. MAXENT Premature – ST. MAXENT – LONQUEMORT – QREBAULT MESNIL – ARBRE – TRINQUIS – ONICOURT Decauntine – TOURSEN – VIMEU – HOUDEN Present Brigade signal office taken over with their lines to TOURS – EN – VIMEU OISEMONT and a return of their line ERCOURT – VISMES ENVAL. Communications by telephone established as per attached diagram.	

Army Form C. 2118.

WAR DIARY
or
INTELLIGENCE SUMMARY
(Erase heading not required.)

Instructions regarding War Diaries and Intelligence Summaries are contained in F. S. Regs., Part II. and the Staff Manual respectively. Title pages will be prepared in manuscript.

Hour, Date, Place	Summary of Events and Information	Remarks and references to Appendices
February 1916 ERCOURT 6th	O.C. Signal Troop received HHQ x in corps for attachment to infantry signals for a period of 3 weeks. Strength 1h Warrant Officer, 1 Officer, 4 Sjts, 2 Cpls as O. Sjts, troops for that period.	
7th – 17th 7th	No change. Training Regimental signallers.	
	Test (Classification) of Permanent signallers. Result attached.	
17th – 27th 25th	No change	
	Capt Campbell reported from attachment to 1st Cav. Sis Regt returned to 9th Hussars at	
27th	No change	

O.P. 9
19/2/16

DIAGRAM OF COMMUNICATIONS.

SECUNDERABAD CAVALRY BRIGADE.

19-2-16

Ref Sheet 11. 1/80,000. ABBEVILLE.

— · — · — Comic Air Line.
· · · · · · · D.I. Cable.
～～～～ D.R. to all units.

Bde H.Q.
Sqdn H.Q.
Office
Residence

VÉRCOURT.

HQ. 2nd D. Horse

Tours-en-
Vimeu.

HAPICOURT
○ D.H.

LONGUE MORT.
HQ. 34th P. Horse

MARTAINNEVILLE.
Bde H.Q. Sqdn.

Arbre Tranquis.
(Sqdn P.H.)

○ HUPPY.

GREBAULT.
MESNIL.

○ ONICOURT.
(Sqdn P.H.)

○ ST MARENT.
(Sqdn P.H.(a))

○ CERISY.
HQ. 7th D. Gds.

V.I.B.
OISEMONT.

D Pipe Lieut

Every Signal Touch
About Low Bde.

SERIAL NO. 247.

Confidential

War Diary

of

Signal Troop, Secunderabad Cavalry Brigade.

FROM 1st March 1916 TO 31st March 1916.

WAR DIARY
or
INTELLIGENCE SUMMARY

Army Form C. 2118.

Hour, Date, Place	Summary of Events and Information	Remarks and references to Appendices
March 1st 1916. ERCOURT. 31st	During this month no change and nothing of note occurred. Communication of the Brigade as for February. A class of the nos 4 and 7 of the machine gun apparatus was formed in which 1st and 2nd Nos of the Signal Troop proceeded daily from 2–4 (Saturdays excepted) training three men in Semaphore. Progress by end of month fair. Training of team of four men in rapid laying and reeling up of cable (mounted) was carried out by base Sig St. (Sgt Harris 4 Terrier 1st D Sqn 3 Terrier, Porventure 2 Terrier Deacon H Stearn). A competition between the teams was held at	

Army Form C. 2118.

Instructions regarding War Diaries and Intelligence Summaries are contained in F. S. Regs., Part II. and the Staff Manual respectively. Title pages will be prepared in manuscript.

WAR DIARY
or
INTELLIGENCE SUMMARY
(Erase heading not required.)

Hour, Date, Place	Summary of Events and Information	Remarks and references to Appendices
	was won by the Decces (Anne Team. This team representing the brigade in the Divisional competition.	
	Two L.A.R. Officers were attached to the Signal Troop on March 20th to complete a three months course (principally of which they had done 5 weeks with S.C.C. Signal Squadron. Training carried out daily.	
30th March	One squadron of Lancashire Hussars (Divl Cavalry 3rd Division) joined Brigade for Training - Billets in ATHEUX. Communication by temporary Telephone line.	

W.J.Campbell Capt.
O.C. Signal Troop S.L.B.

SERIAL NO. 247

Confidential
War Diary
of

Signal Troop, Secunderabad Cavalry Brigade.

FROM 1st July 1916 TO 31st July 1916.

WAR DIARY or INTELLIGENCE SUMMARY

Army Form C. 2118.

(Erase heading not required.)

Instructions regarding War Diaries and Intelligence Summaries are contained in F.S. Regs., Part II. and the Staff Manual respectively. Title pages will be prepared in manuscript.

Hour, Date, Place	Summary of Events and Information	Remarks and references to Appendices
July 1st 3 a.m.	Marched down from BUSSY-LES-DAOURS to a position of assembly just S. of BUIRE, to be ready to seize any opportunity for cavalry action which might be offered by a successful infantry attack. Reconnaissances pushed forward N and E of Méaulte.	
5 p.m.	Brigade moved back to bivouac in BUSSY-LES-DAOURS there being no favourable opportunity for cooperation in the attack.	
July 2nd 5 - 12th	Bivouac BUSSY-LES-DAOURS. Nothing of note. Training of signallers and despatch riders carried out. Three parties of signallers sent out to bring certain cross roads & other approach routes under fire for the cavalry in the event of an advance. During the night of the 12th-13th the brigade	
12th		

WAR DIARY or INTELLIGENCE SUMMARY

Army Form C. 2118.

(Erase heading not required.)

Instructions regarding War Diaries and Intelligence Summaries are contained in F. S. Regs., Part II. and the Staff Manual respectively. Title pages will be prepared in manuscript.

Hour, Date, Place	Summary of Events and Information	Remarks and references to Appendices
July 12th	Marched to a bivouac just S.W. of MEAULTE to be ready to cooperate in the operations which were to commence at 4 am on 14th.	
13th	Bivouac MÉAULTE – lines of approach to position of readiness reconnoitred. Communications by D.R.	
14th 2 am	At 2 am on 14th the brigade moved into position to a position of readiness just E. of BRAY	
4.30 AM	The 7th Dragoon Gds. moved forward to the valley S.E. of MONTAUBAN to act as adv guard to the brigade. Bgde. and Bde Major proceeded to adv Divl H.Q. at BONFRAY FARM (dug in just E.(this)). To maintain communication between these two advanced points of the brigade & the main body a motor cyclist accompanied by Sgts & 1 km in CAFTET WOOD where a relay post of 3 mounted orderlies (Dragoons) and the	

WAR DIARY
or
INTELLIGENCE SUMMARY

(Erase heading not required.)

Army Form C. 2118.

Hour, Date, Place	Summary of Events and Information	Remarks and references to Appendices
July 14th	matter - cyclist was formed. Information from Bde was sent via Fini along road to Gore at BONFRAY FARM day and night. Orders given Bgrs to main body of the bgade sent by motorcyclist attached to Bde Major.	
7 am	Mainbody of brigade moved up to position just W of BONFRAY FARM. 7th Bgs still in valley S of MONTAUBAN. Communication normal (Tel) + DR (mtd)	
9 am	Information received that infantry attack had been successful, our secondaries Bde was ordered forward to cooperate with infantry in attack in right. No 1 and 2 to act as adv guard to the 21st Div. Cav Divn 7th Bgs ordered (verbally 2 a bpy) to man the trenches N of MONTAUBAN and advance to HIGHT No 1 sending patrols mr to both flanks. Remainder of brigade to Phine into the valley just S	

WAR DIARY or INTELLIGENCE SUMMARY

Army Form C. 2118.

(Erase heading not required.)

Instructions regarding War Diaries and Intelligence Summaries are contained in F. S. Regs., Part II. and the Staff Manual respectively. Title pages will be prepared in manuscript.

Hour, Date, Place	Summary of Events and Information	Remarks and references to Appendices
14th July	@ MONTAUBAN. 7th Bgde advance to our hunches in valley S/MONTAUBAN and while brigade became concentrated in valley S/Montauban. Received order about 12 noon a message from Signals 2nd Div inviting me to communicate with STAFF 2nd Bde by means infantry telephone. Reported This A.M. 6.30 Bde and Bdes in attacking infantry — ompnd t per-trough to 2nd Bde. Infantry artillery have all my completed wiring to retain operations very still in progress — 9 miles there nothing out or not possible and were a line which I had commenced to lay in the valley for me (?) RA 2nd Bde to be continued North to 3rd Brit Adv HQ where STAFF 2nd JCD were located). This line proved valuable + should have been laid earlier by the higher formation to the Bde + not by the Bde to the higher formation N.B. It superseded all the cable carried by the Signal Troops	

WAR DIARY
INTELLIGENCE SUMMARY

Army Form C. 2118.

Hour, Date, Place	Summary of Events and Information	Remarks and references to Appendices
14th July	Forward of 7th Wheln. At 5:30 p.m. orders received for We Len Fermathere to cooperate in infantry attack in High Wood. It the place is open left. Telephone with him broken. In min- We hope enemy Formature shown a delay for information coming in by DRs from Division. [illeg] 144 Wood, and reinforcements for with remainder of Troop. Brigade jellyped to S.W.S.T. Cot's E where flew were involved. That redul were invested. Saw S.10 central who relates report enter. Brigade moves W to attack + Staff Signal Troop attempts to reach S.10. central men who SUBSEQUENTLY-found but it was found that S.W. central was too far	

advanced to report centre which was eventually
established in the ridge was × dues 1/BAZENTIN
LE GRAND, whence visual signal by lamp was
opened to MONTAUBAN ridge. See the want
of the cable laid by the troop in the MONTAUBAN
valley was felt as if a cable could have been
laid from ridge down through Cazentin to
position taken up by 2nd Br Division
(for also being used) communications would
have been good during whole night. As it
was mounted gallopers had real difficulty
in finding Bn's brigade [?] report centre
and vice versa. Communication to Div HQ

WAR DIARY
or
INTELLIGENCE SUMMARY

Army Form C. 2118.

(Erase heading not required.)

Hour, Date, Place	Summary of Events and Information	Remarks and references to Appendices
1st July 14	would have been of no better if they (D.W.) had tried to keep from MONTAUBAN. As it was their dumps were fired up by us, both gunners who transmitted by telephone). Communication with intact aeroplanes etc:- Div:- Three aeroplanes were sent and tried to communicate with brigade and did not have extreme communication with I Corp by lamp, but the result is problem of the brigade were ignorant of any call or methods by which to communicate with aeroplane this the manner in which subsequently made to be seen prior to 14th the communication with aeroplanes might have been quite useful	

Army Form C. 2118.

WAR DIARY
or
INTELLIGENCE SUMMARY

(Erase heading not required.)

Instructions regarding War Diaries and Intelligence Summaries are contained in F. S. Regs., Part II. and the Staff Manual respectively. Title pages will be prepared in manuscript.

Hour, Date, Place	Summary of Events and Information	Remarks and references to Appendices
July 15.16 4 a.m.	Brigade moved back from High Wood ridge via valley S.of MONTAUBAN to bivouacs at	
24th & 25th — 31.7.15	MÉAULTE. moved thence to Bivouac BUSSY Bivouac — nothing to report.	

M. Campbell Capt
ct. Signals Section 7 Bde

31.7.16

SERIAL No. 241.

Confidential

War Diary

of

Signal Troop, Secunderabad Cavalry Brigade.

FROM 1st August 1916 TO 31st August 1916.

WAR DIARY
or
INTELLIGENCE SUMMARY

Army Form C. 2118.

August

(Erase heading not required.)

Hour, Date, Place	Summary of Events and Information	Remarks and references to Appendices
August 1st – 7th 1916 BUSSY-LES-DAOURS	Brigade in bivouac at Bussy working parties with 3rd and 15th Corps. Nothing to note. Officers duties recommenced. Lt Marriott 7th Dgs. 2/Lts Strahan (7th Dg.) Pilcher (P.H.) Markham (D4) joined troop for instruction.	
8th August	Brigade marched to MHAINES via AMIENS halting at former place night of 8th-9th.	
9th Aug.	Brigade marched AIRAINES – area NESLE-NORMANDEUSE - PIERRECOURT in the BRESLE river.	
10th Aug. ↓ 16th Aug.	Billets NESLE-NORMANDEUSE. Training of Brigade – Young signallers. Communication ridden by mile with 2nd Ind Cav Div (harassment fire on an elongy). Also by wire to all units (communication in permanent lines.)	

Army Form C. 2118.

WAR DIARY
or
INTELLIGENCE SUMMARY

(Erase heading not required.)

Hour, Date, Place	Summary of Events and Information	Remarks and references to Appendices
August 1916.	Diagram of communications (by telephone) in the NESLE-NORMANDEUSE area.	

Rieux (VIB) — Blangy — Nesle-Normandeuse (PII) — Bourbel (MG) — Guiverville (UN)

Hierval — Pierrecourt (CDO) (CD)

WAR DIARY
or
INTELLIGENCE SUMMARY

Army Form C. 2118.

(Erase heading not required.)

Instructions regarding War Diaries and Intelligence Summaries are contained in F. S. Regs., Part II. and the Staff Manual respectively. Title pages will be prepared in manuscript.

Hour, Date, Place	Summary of Events and Information	Remarks and references to Appendices
August 1916		
16th August	Brigade marched to RIENCOURT-LÆHIESYE.	
17th August	" " " BUSSY-LES-DAOURS.	
18th — 28th	Brigade in bivouac + billets. BUSSY-LES-DAOURS with working parties detached to H.Q. & Corps Communication with Tramp parties established by a line through 2CO (Cam Corps Squads) — 4th Army — depôt. H.Q. digging party employed by a line to that Office BECOURT also. Also two D.R.'s attached by Divn. to working parties called at 10 a.m. H.Q. BUSSY daily Communication book 2 27 I/CD by wire through 2CO + 4th Army + Corps. (Cards spoke on Tel. line). Also by D.R.'s meeting at MOLLIENS VIDAME at 3 p.m. Daily. Also by D.R.'s through 4th Army + Corps. (Runner to Hospital & two Wm.)
29th	Brigade marched to MOLLIENS VIDAME. Two Officers, under instn. Team ordered to join them by SqDn on 31st.	
30th	Brigade marched MOLLIENS to BRESLE and so upon.	
31st	Lts. MADDUIT + STAUBEN posted to Signal Squadron 2nd I/CD	

Army Form C. 2118.

WAR DIARY
or
INTELLIGENCE SUMMARY

(Erase heading not required.)

Hour, Date, Place	Summary of Events and Information	Remarks and references to Appendices
August 31st	Orders from X corps Signals to convert line 211 - Mq - UN from Enstis circuit to metallic army to interference and induction from it on W.13 - NEO line. Photos issued out.	

M.B.Hampstead
Capt.
O/C Signal Troop
Redoubt / nr. Bde
31.8.16

SERIAL NO. 247.

Confidential Diary of

Signal Troop, Secunderabad Cavalry Brigade.

FROM 1st September 1916 TO 30th September 1916.

Legbd. Bde.
Signal Troop Vol III

WAR DIARY
or
INTELLIGENCE SUMMARY

Army Form C. 2118.

Hour, Date, Place	Summary of Events and Information	Remarks and references to Appendices
September 1916		
NESLE-NORMANDEUSE 1st – 5th	Nothing to report. Signal Troop in billets and bivouac. Communications by telephone to all units. (see Diagram for August).	
6th	Brigade marched to OISSY. Billets + bivouacs night at OISSY and RIENCOURT. Signal HQ. in chateau OISSY.	
7th	Brigade marched to BUSSY-LES-DAOURS.	
7th – 14th	Bivouac BUSSY	
14th	Marched to position of readiness at MAMETZ	
14th – 17th	Remained at MAMETZ – nothing to report.	
17th	Returned to bivouac at BUSSY	
17th – 26th	BUSSY – nothing to report.	
26th	Marched to OISSY + remained in billets + bivouac there till 29th.	
29th	Marched to ST. PIERRE A GOUY - last here to revisit at CROUY.	

McCammon Captⁿ. O. Signal Troop.

1247 W 3299 300,000 (E) 8/14 J.B.C. & A. Forms/C. 2118/11.

SERIAL NO. 247.

Confidential
War Diary
of

Signal Troop, 9th Secunderabad Cavalry Brigade.

FROM 1st October 1916 TO 31st October 1916
30th November

Army Form C. 2118.

WAR DIARY
or
INTELLIGENCE SUMMARY

Signal Troop Sec?? (cav B??)

(Erase heading not required.)

Instructions regarding War Diaries and Intelligence Summaries are contained in F. S. Regs., Part II. and the Staff Manual respectively. Title Pages will be prepared in manuscript.

Place	Date	Hour	Summary of Events and Information	Remarks and references to Appendices
ST. PIERRE A GOUY	1st October		At bivouac and billets ST. PIERRE À GOUY. Nothing special to report. Training of signallers & communication schemes carried out. Diagram of communications attached.	
	31st October	10/10		

2449 Wt. W14957/M90 750,000 1/16 J.B.C. & A. Forms/C.2118/12.

Diagram of Communications
Second Canadian Bde
at St. Pierre-à-Gouy
October 1916

Piano House   Dugan House
   (CC)   (CBO)
    ⊙-----------⊙----------------.
                                  |
GROUY.   Machine Gun Sqdn
                         (MG)
                          ⊙
                          |
                          |
                     Bde Office
                        ⊙----⊙ 75 Dragon Pt
                       / ⊙⊙ \   (T.1)
                      ⊙   ⊙   ⊙
                    ST. PIERRE
                     À GOUY
                      PI. exchange
                              ·
                               ·
                                ·-----·-----·-----·-----·-----⊙ 127 I.C.D.
                                                               (VIB).

·········· german wire (tunnelled)
——— field improvement lin.
— · — · — air line (Curtis).

N.K. Campbell   Captain
               or Signal Subaltern
                            Bde

Signal Troop

5th Cavy Bde.

War Diary

From 1st November to 30th November 1916

Vol. V

Army Form C. 2118.

WAR DIARY
or
INTELLIGENCE SUMMARY

(Erase heading not required.)

Instructions regarding War Diaries and Intelligence Summaries are contained in F. S. Regs., Part II. and the Staff Manual respectively. Title Pages will be prepared in manuscript.

Place	Date	Hour	Summary of Events and Information	Remarks and references to Appendices
FEUQUIERES	Mons 1st		Brigade marched from ST. PIERRE À GOUY via AIRAINES and OISEMONT to the area FEUQUIERES - AIGNEVILLE - MAISNIERES - BUIGNY LES GAMACHES -	
	2nd		Batt. Hqrs. and Signal Troop billeted in FEUQUIERES	
	6th		Construction of temporary cable lines connecting up AIGNEVILLE - HOCQUELUS - BUIGNY and HARCELAINES to Signal Office in FEUQUIERES. Officers class (this from 7th Bgde, one from Pomerania, one from Deccan Horse) commenced work.	
	7th		Nothing to report.	
	21/st			
	22nd		Construction of "ommieain lines" to replace cable lines, according to attached diagram.	
	30th		Officers class daily 9-12 & 5-7.30	

W. G. Campbell
Capt.
O.C. Signal Troop Secunderabad Cav. Bgde.

Diagram of Communications
Secunderabad Cav. Bde.   Nov 30th 1916:

- Bde office
- 1st Mess
- 7th Dragoon Guards
- Secunderabad Cav. Bde. exchange
- Poona Horse. Aigneville.
- Machine gun Sqn. Buigny-lès-gamaches
- Deccan Horse. Havrelaines
- 5th Cav. Div. Exchange

SERIAL NO. 24.1.

Confidential
War Diary
of

Signal Troop, Secunderabad Cavalry Brigade.

FROM 1st December 1916 TO 31st December 1916

WAR DIARY
or
INTELLIGENCE SUMMARY

Army Form C. 2118.

Received 6ow Bde
Signal Troop
Vol VI

Place	Date	Hour	Summary of Events and Information	Remarks and references to Appendices
Fauquière	1st to 24th December		Nothing to report. Training of signallers & Officers clean & building & maintaining permanent lines in Bde area.	
	24th		10 O.R.'s arrived from Signal Depôt to replace Indians. x	
	24th to 31st		Training of new men. (Riding school & stable duties). Communications for December as per diagram submitted with November Diary	

W Campbell
Capt.

BEF

2 IND. CAV. DIV.

SECUNDERABAD BDE.

Bde Machine Gun Sqd

1916 FEB to 1916 DEC

SECUNDERABAD CAVALRY Brigade M.G. Squadron   Army Form C. 2118.

WAR DIARY
or
INTELLIGENCE SUMMARY.

(Erase heading not required.)

From 1-3-16 to 31-3-16

Instructions regarding **War** Diaries and Intelligence Summaries are contained in F. S. Regs., Part II, and the Staff Manual respectively. Title pages will be prepared in manuscript.

Hour, Date, Place.	Summary of Events and Information.	Remarks and references to Appendices.
MARTAINNEVILLE. 1-3-16.	2 Section Gun firing. 4 Sections mounted drill.	Ref. Map. ABBEVILLE 1:80,000.
2-3-16.	Horse Exercise. Revolver Competition - Officers versus N.C.O's.	
3-3-16.	Training under Section Commanders.	
4-3-16.	Training under Section Commanders. Transport parade under the whole.	
5-3-16.	Sunday.	
6-3-16.	Parades cancelled on account of snow.	
7-3-16.	Training under Section Commanders. G.O.C's inspection of Recruits.	
8-3-16.	Inspection of 2 Sections in marching order. 4 Sections training under Section Commanders.	
9-3-16.	Inspection of M.G. Squadron in marching order by G.O.C.	
10-3-16.	Training under Section Commanders.	
11-3-16.	Training under Section Commanders.	
12-3-16.	Church Parade.	
13-3-16.	Handy Order Parade of M.G. Squadron.	

Army Form C. 2118.

WAR DIARY
or
INTELLIGENCE SUMMARY.
(Erase heading not required.)

From 8-2-16 to 29-2-16.

Instructions regarding War Diaries and Intelligence Summaries are contained in F. S. Regs., Part II, and the Staff Manual respectively. Title pages will be prepared in manuscript.

Hour, Date, Place.	Summary of Events and Information.	Remarks and references to Appendices.
St. MAXENT 8-2-16	Machine Gun Squadron formed. 5 Sections billeted in St MAXENT. 1 Section billeted in MARTAINNEVILLE.	Ref. Map :- ABBEVILLE 1:80000.
9-2-16	Settled down into billets. Several horses in the open. Heavy fall of snow last night.	
10-2-16	Drill of Sections under Section Commanders.	
11-2-16	Parade cancelled owing to very bad weather.	
12-2-16	Horse Exercise. 1 Officer, 2 NCO's & men went to Machine Gun Course at WISQUES.	
13-2-16	Sunday.	
14-2-16	Divisional Field day. M.G. Squadron paraded at St MAXENT at 9-30 a.m. Returned to billets at about 4.0 p.m. Heavy storm about 2 p.m.	
15-2-16	Parade under Section Commanders. 2 Sections to Musketry Gun firing.	
16-2-16	Parade cancelled on account of weather. 9 NCO's & men returned from M. G. shoot at NORMANDEUSE.	
17-2-16	Parades under Section Commanders.	
18-2-16	Horse Exercise.	
19-2-16	Machine Gun Squadron less one Section (billeted in MARTAINNEVILLE) moved into billets at MARTAINNEVILLE.	

SECUNDERABAD CAVALRY Brigade M.G. Squadron

Army Form C. 2118.

WAR DIARY
or
INTELLIGENCE SUMMARY.

(Erase heading not required.)

From 1-3-16 to 31-3-16

Instructions regarding War Diaries and Intelligence Summaries are contained in F.S. Regs., Part II, and the Staff Manual respectively. Title pages will be prepared in manuscript.

Hour, Date, Place.	Summary of Events and Information.	Remarks and references to Appendices.
MARTAINNEVILLE 1-3-16.	2 Section Gun firing. 4 Sections mounted drill.	Ref. Map. ABBEVILLE 1:80,000.
2-3-16.	Horse Exercise. Revolver Competition - Officers versus N.C.O's.	
3-3-16.	Training under Section Commanders.	
4-3-16.	Training under Section Commanders. Transport parade under the shelter.	
5-3-16.	Sunday.	
6-3-16.	Parades cancelled on account of snow.	
7-3-16.	Training under Section Commanders. G.O.C.'s inspection of Remounts.	
8-3-16.	Inspection of 2 Sections in marching order. 4 Section to Hornoy under Section Commander.	
9-3-16.	Inspection of M.G. Squadron in Marching Order by G.O.C.	
10-3-16.	Training under Section Commander.	
11-3-16.	Training under Section Commander.	
12-3-16	Church Parade.	
13-3-16.	Brigade Order Parade of M.G. Squadron.	

Army Form C. 2118.

WAR DIARY
or
INTELLIGENCE SUMMARY.

(Erase heading not required.)

From 8-2-16. to 29-2-16.

Instructions regarding War Diaries and Intelligence Summaries are contained in F. S. Regs., Part II, and the Staff Manual respectively. Title pages will be prepared in manuscript.

Hour, Date, Place.	Summary of Events and Information.	Remarks and references to Appendices.
St. MAXENT 8-2-16.	Machine Gun Squadron formed. 5 Sections billeted in St MAXENT. 1 Section billeted in MARTAINNEVILLE.	Ref. Map:- ABBEVILLE 1:80000.
9-2-16.	Settled down into billets. Several horses in the open.	
10-2-16.	Heavy fall of snow last night. Drill of Sections under Section Commanders.	
11-2-16.	Parade cancelled owing to very bad weather.	
12-2-16.	Horse Exercise. 1 officer, 2 NCO's + men went to Machine Gun Course at WISQUES.	
13-2-16	Sunday.	
14-2-16.	Divisional Field day. M.G. Squadron paraded at St MAXENT at 9-30 am. Returned to billets at about 4 o'pm. Heavy storm about 2 pm.	
15-2-16.	Parade under Section Commanders. 2 Sections to burst + Gun firing.	
16-2-16.	Parade cancelled on account of weather. 9 NCO's + men returned from M.G. School at NORMANDEUSE.	
17-2-16.	Parades under Section Commanders.	
19-2-16.	Horse Exercise.	
19-2-16.	Machine Gun Squadron less one Section (billeted in MARTAINNEVILLE) moved into billets at MARTAINNEVILLE.	

Army Form C. 2118.

WAR DIARY
or
INTELLIGENCE SUMMARY.

(Erase heading not required.)

Instructions regarding War Diaries and Intelligence Summaries are contained in F. S. Regs., Part II, and the Staff Manual respectively. Title pages will be prepared in manuscript.

Hour, Date, Place.	Summary of Events and Information.	Remarks and references to Appendices.
20-2-16.	Church Parade at 11-0 am.	
21-2-16.	Received transport for Machine Gun Squadron from ABBEVILLE.	
22-2-16.	Parades under Section Commander.	
23-2-16.	Training under Section Commander. 2 Section gun firing.	
24-2-16.	Parades cancelled owing to bad weather.	
25-2-16.	" " " " (snow).	
26-2-16.	" " " " "	
27-2-16.	Sunday.	
28-2-16.	Parades cancelled owing to bad weather & snow.	
29-2-16.	Training under Section Commander. 2 Section gun firing.	

E. Chatton. Capt.
O.C. Machine Gun Squadron
Sec. Cav. Bde.

Army Form C. 2118.

WAR DIARY
or
INTELLIGENCE SUMMARY.

(Erase heading *not required*.)

Instructions regarding War Diaries and Intelligence Summaries are contained in F. S. Regs., Part II, and the Staff Manual respectively. Title pages will be prepared in manuscript.

Hour, Date, Place.	Summary of Events and Information.	Remarks and references to Appendices.
14-3-16.	Practice for Divisional Competition Semaphore drill -	
15-3-16.	Drill of M.G. Squadron.	
16-3-16.	Meeting Order Parade of two sections & Section Troop under Section Commander.	
17-3-16.	Horse and Parade. Semaphore drill -	
18-3-16.	Training under Section Commander. Compass practice -	
19-3-16.	Sunday -	
20-3-16.	Training for Divisional Competition Gun drill - Semaphore drill -	
21-3-16.	Training for Divisional Competition Semaphore drill -	
22-3-16.	Training for Divisional Competition Semaphore drill.	
23-3-16.	Inspection by G.O.C. cancelled owing to bad weather.	

Army Form C. 2118.

WAR DIARY
or
INTELLIGENCE SUMMARY.

(Erase heading not required.)

Instructions regarding War Diaries and Intelligence Summaries are contained in F. S. Regs., Part II, and the Staff Manual respectively. Title pages will be prepared in manuscript.

Hour, Date, Place.	Summary of Events and Information.	Remarks and references to Appendices.
24-3-16.	B-de Route March cancelled owing to Snow.	
25-3-16.	Horse Exercise. Transport parade.	
26-3-16.	Sunday.	
27-3-16.	Troop Ldr. Section Comeates. Semaphone drill.	
28-3-16.	Inspection of 2 Sections at 10-0 — by G.O.C.	
29-3-16.	Brigade Route March - Left billets at 8.45 a.m. returned at 1.45 p.m. Divisional boxing Competition.	
30-3-16.	Horse Exercise.	
31-3-16.	Tactical Exercise.	

Elverton Capt.
O.C. M.G. Squadron
Sec. Cav. Bde.

SERIAL NO. 317.

Confidential

War Diary

of

Machine Gun Squadron, Secunderabad Cavalry Brigade.

FROM 1st April 1916 TO 30th April 1916.

Army Form C. 2118.

WAR DIARY
or
INTELLIGENCE SUMMARY.

From 1-4-16 to 30-4-16.

Instructions regarding War Diaries and Intelligence Summaries are contained in F. S. Regs., Part II, and the Staff Manual respectively. Title pages will be prepared in manuscript.

(Erase heading not required.)

Hour, Date, Place.	Summary of Events and Information.	Remarks and references to Appendices.
MARTAINNEVILLE 1-4-16.	Horse Exercise. Transport + Height + Saddle Inspection.	Ref. Map. ABBEVILLE 1 : 20,000.
2-4-16.	Sunday.	
3-4-16.	No 1, 2, 3 + 4 Sections foray. No 5 + 6 Sections training & Section training. No 4 + 7 Semaphore drill.	
4-4-16.	Holiday on account of assumption of office by new Viceroy and G.G. of India.	
5-4-16.	Inspection of translated Machine Gun Section.	
6-4-16.	Horse Exercise.	
7-4-16.	Horse Exercise. Recruit parade at 1-30 p.m.	
8-4-16.	Horse + Transport inspection.	
9-4-16.	Sunday.	
10-4-16.	Ran off M.G. Competition for a 6 hr) Shoot. No 4 + 7 Semaphore drill.	
11-4-16.	Horse Exercise. M.G. team left in to practice for M.G. Competition.	
12-4-16.	Terminal Shoot. 2:45 Recce Section accompt (British) Lt Burk' Section accompt (Indian)	

Army Form C. 2118.

WAR DIARY
or
INTELLIGENCE SUMMARY.

(Erase heading not required.)

Instructions regarding War Diaries and Intelligence Summaries are contained in F. S. Regs., Part II, and the Staff Manual respectively. Title pages will be prepared in manuscript.

Hour, Date, Place.	Summary of Events and Information.	Remarks and references to Appendices.
13-4-16.	Horse Exercise	
14-4-16.	Cleaning up billets + lines. Bde Parade cancelled owing to bad weather.	
15-4-16.	Two Sections worked with R.S.F. Section. Two Sections to training.	
16-4-16.	Gun Inspection. Church Parade.	
17-4-16.	Parade cancelled owing to bad weather.	
18-4-16.	Bde Tactical Exercise.	
19-4-16.	Horse Exercise. Cleaning up of billets preparing to move.	
20-4-16.	The Bde. moved to the area ST RIQUIER, ST MAGUILLE, NEUVILLE ONEUX. Marching via LES CROISETTES, Route NATIONALE N° 28 Eastern outskirts of ABBEVILLE - CA L'ABBAYE to ST RIQUIER. M.G. Squadron billeted at NEUVILLE.	
21-4-16.	M.G. Squadron to Squadron training.	
22-4-16.	M.G. Squadron to Squadron training.	
23-4-16.	M.G. Squadron to Squadron training.	
24-4-16.	Squadron training	

Army Form C. 2118.

WAR DIARY
or
INTELLIGENCE SUMMARY.

(Erase heading not required.)

Instructions regarding War Diaries and Intelligence Summaries are contained in F. S. Regs., Part II, and the Staff Manual respectively. Title pages will be prepared in manuscript.

Hour, Date, Place.	Summary of Events and Information.	Remarks and references to Appendices.
25-4-16.	Bde Training.	
26-4-16	Bde Tactical Exercise	
27-4-16	Bde Tactical Exercise	
28-4-16	Bde Tactical Exercise	
29-4-16.	Bde returned to permanent billets marching via Route NATIONALE No 25. Northern & Western outskirts of ABBEVILLE, ROUROY, MOYENNEVILLE thence to their respective areas.	
30-4-16	Sunday. Voluntary Church Service at MARTAINVILLE.	

Wharton Capt.
C.C.M.G.
Sec. Cav. Bde.

SERIAL NO. 317.

Confidential

War Diary

of

Machine Gun Squadron, Secunderabad Cavalry Brigade

FROM 1st May 1916 TO 31st May 1916.

Army Form C. 2118.

WAR DIARY

Machine Gun Squadron Lee'ed Cav. Bde.

INTELLIGENCE SUMMARY. From 1st May – 31st May 1916.

Instructions regarding **War** Diaries and Intelligence Summaries are contained in F. S. Regs., Part II, and the Staff Manual respectively. Title pages will be prepared in manuscript.

(Erase heading not *required*.)

Hour, Date, Place.		Summary of Events and Information.	Remarks and references to Appendices.
3 May. MARTINNEVILLE. FRANCE		Time of Reveille changed to 5.30 A.M. & Retiring Post Call to 8.15 P.M.	Ref. Map. ABBEVILLE. Sheet 11. 1/80,000
7th " "		4 Sowars of Poona Horse Sections promoted to Acting L/Dafadars	
8th " "		The Squadron Marched from MARTINNEVILLE at 9.0 AM via LES CROISETTES – ROUTE NATIONALE N°28 – Eastern outskirts of MARTAINE – CH. L'ABBAYE to ST RIQUIER and billeted in same. CAINCHY village for Divisional Training. All horses placed under cover.	
9th " CAINCHY		1st day of Divisional Training –	
10th " "		Medical Inspection of the Squadron taken over by M.O. 2nd D. Horse	
13th " "		Last day of Divisional Training –	
14th " "		The Squadron marched back to permanent billets at MARTAINNEVILLE returning by same route as on 8/5/16. Marched at 9.20 AM and arrived at 3.30 P.M. (Horses picketted in the open).	
15th " MARTAINNEVILLE		1 Charger, 4 R.H.S.C. & R.H.I.C. & 1 Draught Horse taken on the strength. All horses placed under factory sheds on account of inc'lemt weather.	
16th " "		Jemadar MUHAMMAD YASIN KHAN, at Reserve, & 2 horses temporary attached to The Squadron from 34th Poona Horse.	
19th " "		Squadron changed billets, moved into area TOEUFFRES – ROGEANT – HQ.	
20th " ROGEANT		7th Guard Section in ROGEANT. Remaining Sections in TOEUFFRES. Armn. Bricklaying – Capt'n. BURT, LT ARRAN & 2/Lt MACAN attended demonstration at 4th Army School. FLIXECOURT	
21st " "		3 R.H.I.C. taken on the strength	
26th " "		4 B.Os. 2 I.Ds. and 6 N.C.Os. attended Gas demonstration at Gerchu near TOURS at 10 AM	Cdj.....
25th " "		2 Dismounted Indian ranks sold to India Yr. 20 T. Horse – 1 R.H.B.C. discharged (A. Livy) promoted L.A/Dafr and 1 Sowar promoted to A/L.Dafr of Poona Horse Sections.	Cd in Com
" " "		4 R.H.B.C. 2 Pack & 1 Draught horse taken on the strength	... Sqn
27th " "		12 Dismounted men of 7 & Guard Sections returned to Imperial to their regiments	for Sqn
31st " "		Divisional Tactical Exercise without troops for O.C. units –	

SERIAL NO. 317.

Confidential
War Diary
of

Machine Gun Squadron, Secunderabad Cavalry Brigade.

FROM 1st June 1916 TO 30th June 1916.

MACHINE GUN SQUADRON
SEC, CAV, BDE.

Army Form C. 2118.

WAR DIARY or **INTELLIGENCE SUMMARY.** From June 1st to 30th 1916.

(Erase heading not required.)

Instructions regarding War Diaries and Intelligence Summaries are contained in F. S. Regs., Part II, and the Staff Manual respectively. Title pages will be prepared in manuscript.

Hour, Date, Place.	Summary of Events and Information.	Remarks and references to Appendices.
ROGEANT – TEUFLES 1-6-16	Squadron training	Ref Map ABBEVILLE 1/80000
2-6-16	Bde moved to new area - Sqd in billets at BELLOY.	
3,4,5,6 -6-16	Squadron training	
7-6-16	Staff ride for all officers	
8-6-16	Bde returned to old billets - Sqd in billets at ROGEANT	
9,10 -6-16	TEUFLES.	
11 -6-16	Sqd training	
	Church Parade	
12,13,14,15 -6-16	Indirect firing	
16 -6-16	Squadron training	
17 -6-16	Sunday	
18 -6-16		
19 -6-16	Squadron training	
20 -6-16		
21 -6-16		
22 -6-16	Bde moved to training area - Sqd billeted in St RIQUIER	
23-6-16	Bde training	
24-6-16	Other training	
25-6-16	Bde Staff ride for all officers	
26-6-16	Bde moved to CAVILLON - Sqd billeted in CAVILLON arrived at 2.00 - 27-6-16.	

MACHINE GUN SQUADRON
SEC. CAV. BDE.

Army Form C. 2118.

WAR DIARY
or
INTELLIGENCE SUMMARY.

(Erase heading not required.)

Instructions regarding **War** Diaries and Intelligence Summaries are contained in F. S. Regs., Part II, and the Staff Manual respectively. Title pages will be prepared in manuscript.

Hour, Date, Place.	Summary of Events and Information.	Remarks and references to Appendices.
27-6-16	Bde moved at 6-45 to area at BUSSY-LES-DAOURS Sqd bivouac on the L'HALLUE RIVER.	
28-6-16 } 29-6-16 } 30-6-16 }	In bivouac on the L'HALLUE RIVER	

Wharton Capt
O.C. M.G. Sqd
Sec. Cav. Bde.

SERIAL NO. 311.

Confidential
War Diary
of

Machine Gun Squadron, Secunderabad Cavalry Brigade.

FROM 1st July 1916 TO 31st July 1916.

Army Form C. 2118.

Machine Gun Squadron
2nd Cav. Bde.

WAR DIARY
or
INTELLIGENCE SUMMARY.

(Erase heading not required.)

From July 1st to July 3rd 1916.

Instructions regarding War Diaries and Intelligence Summaries are contained in F. S. Regs., Part II, and the Staff Manual respectively. Title pages will be prepared in manuscript.

Hour, Date, Place.		Summary of Events and Information.	Remarks and references to Appendices.
QUERRIEU	1-7-16	Bde marched to BUIRE-SUR-L'ANCRE at 2-30 am in a position of readiness at 5-30 am returned to old bivouacs at QUERRIEU.	AMIENS 17 Scale 1/100000
	2-7-16	Sunday.	
	3-7-16	) Horse Exercise	
	4-7-16	) Gun drill	
	5-7-16	)	
	6-7-16	)	
	7-7-16	Commanding Officers went round the captured German 1st line trenches South of MAMETZ WOOD & MONTAUBAN.	TRENCH MAP Sheet 57C SW Scale 1/20000 AMIENS 17 Scale 1/100000
	8-7-16	Horse Exercise + Gun drill.	
	9-7-16	Church Parade	
	10-7-16	) Horse Exercise	
	11-7-16	) "	
	12-7-16	) Gun drill	
	13-7-16	Bde marched to MEAULTE at 8-30 am & bivouaced.	
	14-7-16	Bde marched to BRAY at 3-0 am. At 7-0 am moved into the valley SE of MONTAUBAN. No 1 & No 2 Sections joined the 7th Dgn. About 5 am No 3, No 6 Sections joined the 7 Dgns leaving No 5 & No 6 Sections in reserve with Poona Horse. 7 Dgt & steam storm with No 1, 2 & 4 Sections moved off into action on mg U of Infantry between SE corner of HIGH WOOD + about within of mg P 10. Lt. D'A.J.T. HARTLEY killed, wounded 9 BR - 1 K.W.R. - Horses 13 killed, 13 wounded.	TRENCH MAP Sheet 62D NE Scale 1/20000
	15-7-16	The Bde moved out of action at 3-30 am, has taken over by Infantry. Marched back to MEAULTE to bivouac.	

Gulab Singh & Sons, Calcutta—No. 22 Army C.—5-8-14—1,07,000.

Army Form C. 2118.

WAR DIARY
or
INTELLIGENCE SUMMARY.

(Erase heading not required.)

Instructions regarding **War** Diaries and Intelligence Summaries are contained in F. S. Regs., Part II, and the Staff Manual respectively. Title pages will be prepared in manuscript.

Hour, Date, Place.	Summary of Events and Information.	Remarks and references to Appendices.
16-7-16.	Sunday noted.	
17-7-16	⎫	
18-7-16	⎬ Horse Exercise	
19-7-16	⎪	
20-7-16	⎭	
21-7-16	Horse Exercise + Gun drill.	
22-7-16	Horse Exercise + Gun drill. Lt ANSON joined the Squadron	
23-7-16	Bde marched back to the bivouacs of QUERRIEU	AMIENS 17 Scale 1/100000
24-7-16	Horse Exercise; show tents.	
25-7-16	G.O.C. of Bde inspected Transport.	
26-7-16	Parades under Section Commanders.	
27-7-16	G.O.C. inspected horses at Stables.	
28-7-16	Parades under Section Commanders.	
29-7-16	Horse Show.	
30-7-16	Sunday.	
31-7-16	Horse Exercise - All blankets being fumigated.	

E Chatters Capt
OC. M.G. Sqd.

SERIAL NO. 317.

Confidential
War Diary
of

Machine Gun Squadron Secunderabad Cavalry Brigade.

FROM 1st August 1916 TO 31st August 1916

Machine Gun Squadron
Suc. Cav. Bde.

Army Form C. 2118.

WAR DIARY
or
INTELLIGENCE SUMMARY.

(Erase heading not required.)

from August 1st to 31st 1916.

Instructions regarding War Diaries and Intelligence Summaries are contained in F. S. Regs., Part II, and the Staff Manual respectively. Title pages will be prepared in manuscript.

Place	Hour, Date	Summary of Events and Information.	Remarks and references to Appendices.
QUERRIEU	1-8-16. 2-8-16.	Squadron training under Section Commanders.	Ref. Map AMIENS 1/100000.
	3-8-16	Bde. Staff Ride.	
	4-8-16	Squadron training	
	5-8-16		
	6-8-16.	Church Parade	
	7-8-16.	Squadron training	
	8-8-16.	Bde. moved via DAOURS – AMIENS – PICQUIGNY – SOUES & AIRAINES – M. Sqdt. billeted in Le HAMEL.	Ref. Map ABBEVILLE 1/80000.
	9-8-16.	Bde. moved via ALLERY – NOIREL – OISEMONT – FOUCAUCOURT – area GUNNERVILLE – PIERRECOURT – NESLE NORMANDEUSE – L/Sgt. killed at BOUREL.	
	10-8-16.	Horse Exercise moved camp onto better ground.	
	11-8-16.	G.O.C. inspected the camp.	
	12-8-16	Squadron training.	
	13-8-16	Church Parade.	
	14-8-16	G.O.C. also inspected horses + camp.	
	15-8-16	Squadron training & gun drill.	
	16-8-16	Tactical Scheme without troops.	
	17-8-16	" " with troops.	
	18-8-16	" " troops.	
	19-8-16	Squadron training.	

Army Form C. 2118.

WAR DIARY
or
INTELLIGENCE SUMMARY.
(Erase heading not required.)

Instructions regarding War Diaries and Intelligence Summaries are contained in F. S. Regs., Part II, and the Staff Manual respectively. Title pages will be prepared in manuscript.

Hour, Date, Place.	Summary of Events and Information.	Remarks and references to Appendices.
20-8-16	Sunday.	
21-8-16	G.O.C. inspected horses & carts.	
22-8-16	Squadron training, firing, 1" & 3" drill.	
23-8-16		
24-8-16		
25-8-16	Lectures, Exercise.	
26-8-16	Squadron training, firing & 9" drill.	
27-8-16	Sunday.	
28-8-16	Squadron training.	
29-8-16		
30-8-16		
31-8-16		

Ellwhahn Capt.
O.C. M.G. Sqdt.
Sec. Cav. Bde.

SERIAL NO. 317.

Confidential
War Diary
of

Machine Gun Squadron, Secunderabad Cavalry Brigade.

FROM 1st September 1916 TO 30th September 1916.

Army Form C. 2118.

WAR DIARY
or
INTELLIGENCE SUMMARY.

(Erase heading not required.)

Vol III of Machine Gun Squadron
2nd Ind. Cav. Bde.
from Sept 1st to 30th 1916.

Instructions regarding War Diaries and Intelligence Summaries are contained in F. S. Regs., Part II, and the Staff Manual respectively. Title pages will be prepared in manuscript.

Hour, Date, Place.		Summary of Events and Information.	Remarks and references to Appendices.
BOURBEL	1-9-16 2-9-16	Training under Section Commanders.	Ref. Map DIEPPE 16 Sed. 1/100000
	3-9-16	Church parade.	
	4-9-16	Divisional Sports.	
	5-9-16.	Training under Section Commanders.	
OISSY	6-9-16.	Bde. moved up to OISSY area. marching via SENARPONT – ANDAINVILLE – HORNOY – CAMPS-EN-AMIENOIS – MOLLIENS VIDAME –	Ref. Map. AMIENS 17 Sed. 1/150000
BUSSY	7-9-16	Bde. moved at 2.0am to BUSSY-LES-DAOURS area. marching via FLIXECOURT – BRIQUEMESNIL – FERRIERES – SAVEUSE – AMIENS –	
	8-9-16 9-9-16 10-9-16 11-9-16 12-9-16 13-9-16	Squadron training	
MEAULTE MAMETZ WOOD	14-9-16 15-9-16 16-9-16	Bde. moved at 8.0am to MEAULTE – marching via LA-NEUVILLE – BONNAY – TREUX Bde. moved at 4.30am to MAMETZ WOOD Bde. arrived at MAMETZ WOOD Hostilities...	Ref. Map. Shut 57c Sed. 1/40000
BUSSY	17-9-16 18-9-16 19-9-16 20-9-16 21-9-16 22-9-16 23-9-16 24-9-16	Bde. moved back to BUSSY-LES-DAOURS area. Training under Section Commanders.	Ref Map AMIENS 17 Sed. 1/100000

Army Form C. 2118.

WAR DIARY
or
INTELLIGENCE SUMMARY.

(Erase heading not required.)

Instructions regarding War Diaries and Intelligence Summaries are contained in F. S. Regs., Part II, and the Staff Manual respectively. Title pages will be prepared in manuscript.

Hour, Date, Place.	Summary of Events and Information.	Remarks and references to Appendices.
25-9-16	Squadron training.	
REINCOURT 26-9-16.	Bde moved back to REINCOURT – moving via AMIENS – St SAUVEUR – AILLY – BREILLY – FOURDRINOY – CAVILLON.	Ref Map AMIENS 1/7 Scale 1/100000
27-9-16 } 28-9-16 }	Squadron training.	
GOUY 29-9-16.	Bde moved to St PIERRE-a-GOUY area.	
30-9-16.	Sqd. training.	

E Wratton Capt
O. M. G. Squadron
Sec. Cav. Bde.

SERIAL NO. 317.

Confidential
War Diary
of

Machine Gun Squadron, Secunderabad Cavalry Brigade.

FROM 1st October 1916 TO 30th November 1916
       31st October

Army Form C. 2118.

Secunderabad Machine Gun Squadron **WAR DIARY** or **INTELLIGENCE SUMMARY.** Oct 1st to 31st 1916.

Instructions regarding War Diaries and Intelligence Summaries are contained in F. S. Regs., Part II, and the Staff Manual respectively. Title pages will be prepared in manuscript.

(Erase heading not required.)

Hour, Date, Place.	Summary of Events and Information.	Remarks and references to Appendices.
LE GARD.		Ref Map AMIENS 1/100000
2-10-16.		
3-10-16		
4-10-16	Squadron training.	
5-10-16		
6-10-16		
7-10-16		
8-10-16		
9-10-16		
10-10-16		
11-10-16		
12-10-16		
13-10-16	Brigade field day.	
14-10-16	Squadron training.	
16-10-16	Brigade field day.	
17-10-16		
18-10-16		
19-10-16	Squadron training.	
20-10-16		
21-10-16		
23-10-16		
24-10-16		
25-10-16		
26-10-16	Capt Bent took over command of 1st M.G. Sqd.	
27-10-16	Hindu Holiday.	
28-10-16		
30-10-16	Squadron training	
31-10-16		

Ellvatson Major
OC. M.G. Sqd. Sec. Cav. Bde.

Machine Gun Squadron
32nd Cavalry Brigade

War Diary

From 1st November 1916 to 30th November 1916

Vol. V

Army Form C. 2118.

WAR DIARY
or
INTELLIGENCE SUMMARY.

from Nov 1st to 30th 1916.
Secunderabad Cavalry Gen Squad

(Erase heading not required.)

Instructions regarding War Diaries and Intelligence Summaries are contained in F. S. Regs., Part II, and the Staff Manual respectively. Title pages will be prepared in manuscript.

Hour, Date, Place.	Summary of Events and Information.	Remarks and references to Appendices.
LE GARD ST PIERRE-A-GOUY 1-11-16.	The Bde marched via AIRAINES - OISEMONT - CERISY - VISMES - FEUQUIRES cross - Secunderabad Cav Sqd billeted in BUIGNY-LES-GAMACHES.	AMIENS 17 Sqdn 1/100000 ABBEVILLE 14 Sqdn 1/100000
2-11-16 3-11-16 4-11-16 6-11-16	Squadron Training	
7-11-16 8-11-16 9-11-16 10-11-16 11-11-16	Squadron Training	
13-11-16 14-11-16 15-11-16 16-11-16 17-11-16 18-11-16	Squadron Training	
19-11-16.	Squadron received Lieuts LISTER-KAYE, STEPHENSON, DEMPERS, FRANCIS & 130 O.R.B. (New War Establishment)	

Army Form C. 2118.

WAR DIARY
or
INTELLIGENCE SUMMARY.

(Erase heading not required.)

Instructions regarding War Diaries and Intelligence Summaries are contained in F. S. Regs., Part II, and the Staff Manual respectively. Title pages will be prepared in manuscript.

Hour, Date, Place.	Summary of Events and Information.	Remarks and references to Appendices.
20-11-16		
21-11-16	All Indian ranks returned to their Regt.	
22-11-16	} Squadron training	
23-11-16		
24-11-16		
25-11-16		
26-11-16	Church parade cancelled bad weather	
27-11-16	Squadron training	
28-11-16	Squadron inspected by G.O.C. Bde in Review Order	
29-11-16	} Squadron training	
30-11-16		

Elwater Major
O.C. M.G. Squadron
Sec. Cav. Bde
II: Ind. Cav. Div.

SERIAL No. 311

Confidential
War Diary
of

Machine Gun Squadron, Lucknow attached Cavalry Brigade.

FROM 1st December 1916 TO 31st December 1916.

Army Form C. 2118.

WAR DIARY from 1st to 31st 1916

INTELLIGENCE SUMMARY. SECUNDERABAD. M.G. Squadron

Vol VI

(Erase heading not required.)

Instructions regarding **War Diaries** and **Intelligence Summaries** are contained in F. S. Regs., Part II, and the Staff Manual respectively. Title pages will be prepared in manuscript.

Hour, Date, Place.	Summary of Events and Information.	Remarks and references to Appendices.
BUIGNY LES GAMACHES		
1/12/16	} Squadron Training	
2/12/16		
3/12/16		
4/12/16		
5/12/16		
6/12/16		
7/12/16		
8/12/16	Inspection by Divisional Commander marching order	
9/12/16		
10/12/16		
11/12/16		
12/12/16		
13/12/16		
14/12/16		
15/12/16		
16/12/16	} Squadron Training	
17/12/16		
18/12/16		
19/12/16		
20/12/16		
21/12/16		
22/12/16		
23/12/16		
24/12/16	x mas day. Major Watson proceeded on 9 months course to Anson Golf course	preliminary

Army Form C. 2118.

WAR DIARY
or
INTELLIGENCE SUMMARY

From, Dec 1st to 31st 1916.

SECUNDERABAD M.G. Squadron.

(*Erase heading not required.*)

Instructions regarding **War** Diaries and Intelligence Summaries are contained in F. S. Regs., Part II, and the Staff Manual respectively. Title pages will be prepared in manuscript.

Hour, Date, Place.	Summary of Events and Information.	Remarks and references to Appendices.
BUIGNY LES GAMACHES. 26/12/16 27/12/16 28/12/16 29/12/16 30/12/16 31/12/16.	} Squadron training.	

T. G. Anson.
Commanding Secunderabad
M.G. Squadron.

BEF

2 Ind. Cav. Div.

Secunderabad Bde

Mobile Vet. Section

1914 Oct — 1916 Dec

Duplicate Copy.

WAR DIARY
OF

Mobile Veterinary Section, Secunderabad Cavalry Brigade

From 28th October 1914 to 31st March 1915

WAR DIARY

of

Mobile Veterinary Section, Secunderabad Cavalry Brigade.

From 28. October 1914 to 7. March 1915.

Mobile Veterinary Section
Documents Cavalry Brigade

Army Form C. 2118.

WAR DIARY
or
INTELLIGENCE SUMMARY
(Erase heading not required.)

Instructions regarding War Diaries and Intelligence Summaries are contained in F.S. Regs., Part II. and the Staff Manual respectively. Title pages will be prepared in manuscript.

Hour, Date, Place	Summary of Events and Information	Remarks and references to Appendices
28/10/14. Camp la Source Orleans	Orders from D.V.S. Allowed to form Mobile Veterinary Section for Brigade. Sanction for personnel to be drawn from base and equipment etc. was obtained as soon as possible.	
29/10/14. " "	Brigade left Orleans. Nucleus of Section left to await arrival of personnel from Base (Marseilles.)	
16/11/14. "	Orders from Base Commandant, Orleans, to rejoin Brigade at once as personnel for section had been sent direct to Brigade.	
19/11/14. "	Obtained orders from D.A.D.R.T. and left Orleans 5 p.m. – arrived Chartres 11 p.m.	
20/11/15	Left Chartres 6 a.m. arrived Rouen 5 p.m.	
21/11/15	Left Rouen 7 p.m.	
22/11/15	Arrived Boulogne 8 a.m. – left Boulogne 11 p.m.	
23/11/15	Arrived Choques 11 a.m. detrained and marched to Bethune, reported to Brigade Headquarters. Took over personnel. Billeted in farm near Bergaste [?] shed quette.	
6/12/15. Bethune	Left Bethune and moved with Brigade to Busnes – again billeted in farm.	
22/12/15. Pont de Balque	Moved to Pont de Balque (Isbergues) – Billeted in school house and yards.	
7/3/15. Neuffoss [?]	Proceded to new billets in large farm at Neuffoss near AIRE.	

1247 W 3260 200,000 (E) 8/14 J.B.C. & A. Forms/C. 2118/11.

Mobile Veterinary Section
[?] Cavalry Brigade

WAR DIARY
or
INTELLIGENCE SUMMARY
(Erase heading not required.)

Army Form C. 2118.

Hour, Date, Place	Summary of Events and Information	Remarks and references to Appendices
26/10/14. Camp de Sauve Orleans.	Orders from D.V.S. Abbeville to form Mobile Veterinary Section for Brigade. Searching for personnel to be drawn from base and equipment to be made available as soon as possible.	
29/10/14. "	Brigade left Orleans. Nucleus of Section left to await arrival of Personnel from Base (Marseilles.)	
18/11/14. "	Orders from Base Commandant, Orleans, to rejoin Brigade at once as personnel for section has been sent direct to Brigade.	
19/11/14. "	Obtained orders from D.A.D.R.T. and left Orleans 5. p.m. – Arrived Chartres 11. p.m.	
20/11/15	Left Chartres 6. a.m. arrived Rouen 5. p.m.	
21/11/15	Left Rouen 7. p.m.	
22/11/15	Arrived Boulogne 8. a.m. – Left Boulogne 11.10 p.m.	
23/11/15	Arrived Choques 11. a.m., detrained and proceeded to Bethune, reported to Brigade Headquarters. Took over personnel. Billets in farm near Brigade Head Quarters.	
6/12/15. Bethune	Left Bethune and moved with Brigade to Busnes – again billets in farm.	
22/12/15. Pont de Balque	Move to Pont de Balque (Isbergues). Billets in school house and yard.	
7/3/15. Neuf[?]	Proceeded to our billet in large farm at Neufpre near AIRE.	

Serial No. 249.

121/6128

WAR DIARY OF

Mobile Veterinary Section, Secunderabad Cavalry Brigade.

From 1st April 1915. To 30th June 1915.

Army Form C. 2118.

WAR DIARY
or
INTELLIGENCE SUMMARY

(Erase heading not required.)

Hour, Date, Place	Summary of Events and Information	Remarks and references to Appendices
7-3-15. NEUFPRÉ	– in camp from near AIRE. On duty as mobilised section. Routine work.	
11-3-15 to 24-4-15	Army Veterinary Corps turnout (11 O.R. Prs) armed for duty with section. Routine work.	
24-4-15	Indian Cavalry Corps under orders to move – got all ready and horses somewhat. Corps moved in direction of Poperinghe – orders received for this section to remain in present billets.	
25-4-15 "	Collected horses left in horses in area evacuated by Cavalry Corps. Routine work	
5-5-15 "	Indian Cavalry Corps returned to its area billeting area – brigades are not Bretts in different parts than those formerly occupied.	
6-5-15 "	Received orders to rejoin brigade in relief by Lucknow Mob. Vet. Veterinary Section	
9-5-15 "	Lucknow M.V. Section took over – we moved out to rejoin brigade and a Lucknow rady to report to Bde. H.Q. – billets in town at Reelinghen	

WAR DIARY
or
INTELLIGENCE SUMMARY

(Erase heading not required.)

Army Form C. 2118.

Instructions regarding War Diaries and Intelligence Summaries are contained in F. S. Regs., Part II, and the Staff Manual respectively. Title pages will be prepared in manuscript.

Hour, Date, Place	Summary of Events and Information	Remarks and references to Appendices
10-5-15. RECLINGHEM.	Routine work.	
14-5-15 "	Received orders from Brigade that in event of move orders to remain in present billets until further orders.	
17-5-15 "	Brigade moved out in direction of ALLOUAGNE. — Greenus and winners horses left temporarily in billets.	
19-5-15 "	Received orders to move out and rejoin Brigade — orders received evening of same not not daylight. — Brand intelligence that Brigade is camping had to follow forced road to [illeg] park.	
20-5-15 "	Received orders and moved into Armee billets in farm at GLEM (Winnie) morning.	
30-5-15 GLEM.	Routine work.	
31-5-15 "	Routine work.	
1-6-15 "	} Routine work	
30-6-15 "		

Serial No. 249.

12/6948

WAR DIARY
OF

Mobile Veterinary Section, Secunderabad Cavalry Brigade.

FROM 1st July 1915 TO 31st August 1915

WAR DIARY
or
INTELLIGENCE SUMMARY

(Erase heading not required.)

Army Form C. 2118

Instructions regarding War Diaries and Intelligence Summaries are contained in F.S. Regs., Part II. and the Staff Manual respectively. Title pages will be prepared in manuscript.

Hour, Date, Place	Summary of Events and Information	Remarks and references to Appendices
1-7-15. G.L.E.M.	Routine work.	
10-7-15. "	Moved into new billets in farm at W and annex.	
11-7-15. Wandonne	Billets in farm at S.W. end of village	
11-7-15 to 31-7-15	Routine work.	
1-8-15. Wandonne	Marched out - rendezvous at Crossroads S.E. of Renescure 10. A.M. proceeded to Brimeux. Billets for night in farm in village.	
2-8-15. Brimeux	Moved on rendezvous at Bois Jean 6.15. proceeded via ABBEVILLE to Bellencourt where billets for night.	
3-8-15. Bellencourt	Moved out. rendezvous at crossroads Bellencourt at 9. a.m. as escorted via Pont Remy - Airaines to Crouy. Billets in farm S.W. of Crouy.	
4-8-15. Crouy.	Routine work	
5-8-15. "		
" Crouy	Changed areas to Sorus.	
6-8-15. Sorus.		
7-8-15 "	Routine work.	
31-8-15 "		

Serial No. 249.

Confidential
121/7601

War Diary

at

Mobile Veterinary Section, Secunderabad Cavalry Brigade.

FROM 1st October 1915. TO (c) 31st October 1915.

Army Form C. 2118.

WAR DIARY
or
INTELLIGENCE SUMMARY

Mobile Veterinary Section, Indicated Cavalry Brigade.

(Erase heading not required.)

Instructions regarding War Diaries and Intelligence Summaries are contained in F. S. Regs., Part II. and the Staff Manual respectively. Title pages will be prepared in manuscript.

Hour, Date, Place	Summary of Events and Information	Remarks and references to Appendices
1-9-15 SOUES.	Routine Work. Received manuals for animals at rate of 1-10% of strength.	
14-9-15 SOUES.	Changed Billet to house of Rouban Notre.	
15-9-15 to 20-9-15 SOUES.	Routine work. Evacuated horses from Rouhues (hongré).	
21-9-15	Moved out – rendezvous at Piéquigny – marched via Viquecourt. Canaples – to GORGES. Bivouacked by field inside village of GORGES.	
22-9-15 to 12-10-15 GORGES	Routine Work – evacuated horses from Raithed (DOULLENS).	
13-10-15 BUSSUS BUSSUE.	Moved to BUSSUS-BUSSUE – Billets in farm in village – Routine work – Evacuated animals direct to ABBEVILLE by rail.	
22-10-15	Moved to PONT REMY – Billets in large farm S.E. of crossroads at eastern entrance to PONT-REMY.	
23-10-15 PONT-REMY.	Routine work. Animals evacuated by road to ABBEVILLE.	
31-10-15		

(8)

Serial No. 249.

77/80/D

Confidential

War Diary

of

Mobile Veterinary Section, Secunderabad Cavalry Brigade.

FROM 1st November 1915 TO 30th November 1915

WAR DIARY

Motor Veh. Workshop. Second enlarged Convoy Brigade

INTELLIGENCE SUMMARY

Army Form C. 2118.

Instructions regarding War Diaries and Intelligence Summaries are contained in F. S. Regs., Part II. and the Staff Manual respectively. Title pages will be prepared in manuscript.

(Erase heading not required.)

Hour, Date, Place		Summary of Events and Information	Remarks and references to Appendices
1-11-15	PONT-REMY	Routine Work.	
5-11-15	" "		
6-11-15	" "		
	ST. MAXENT.	Moved to ST. MAXENT. - Billets in farm.	
7-11-15 to 20-11-15	ST. MAXENT.	Routine work. - Evacuated horses by road to ABBEVILLE.	
20-11-15		Billeting area again changed - moved to LIMEUX - Billets in the farm at W. end of village.	
21-11-15 to 29-11-15	LIMEUX.	Routine work - Got own Mange cases from 34th Prime Horse - Evacuees horses by road to ABBEVILLE. - Dauentwich slattoedic.	
30-11-15	LIMEUX	Routine work.	

SERIAL NO. 249.

Confidential

War Diary

of

Mobile Veterinary Section, Secunderabad Cavalry Brigade.

FROM 1st December 1915 TO 31st December 1915

Army Form C. 2118.

WAR DIARY
or
INTELLIGENCE SUMMARY

Mobile Vety. Section (a) Cavalry Role (b) Cavalry Role

Instructions regarding War Diaries and Intelligence Summaries are contained in F. S. Regs, Part II. and the Staff Manual respectively. Title pages will be prepared in manuscript.

(Erase heading not required.)

Hour, Date, Place	Summary of Events and Information	Remarks and references to Appendices
1-12-15 to 2-12-15 LIMEUX.	Routine work — D.D.V.S. Indian Cavalry Corps orders that all horses known to be unaccustomed will be tested forth Mallein by Intra dermal method. (Vet Matthew).	
3-12-15 LIMEUX.	Received order from A.D.V.S. that A.V.C. personnel are to carry arms — details in Ordnance for rifles.	
4-12-15 5-12-15 LIMEUX.	Routine work.	
6-12-15 LIMEUX.	A.D.V.S. inspected section.	
7-12-15 "	ROUTINE WORK.	
7-12-15 to 16-12-15	Moved to HUPPY. Billeted in farms (x) S.W. Indian Brigade	
17-12-15		
18-12-15 to 31-12-15 HUPPY.	ROUTINE WORK. Brigade tested with Mallein (see annexes) during this period.	
	Number of Animals evacuated to Veterinary Hospital during month 130.	

SERIAL NO. 2447.

Confidential

War Diary

of

Mobile Veterinary Section, Secunderabad Cavalry Brigade.

FROM 1st January 1916 TO 31st January 1916.

Army Form C. 2118.

Mobile Vety. Section
attached Cavalry Brigade

WAR DIARY
or
INTELLIGENCE SUMMARY

(Erase heading not required.)

Instructions regarding War Diaries and Intelligence Summaries are contained in F. S. Regs., Part II. and the Staff Manual respectively. Title pages will be prepared in manuscript.

Hour, Date, Place		Summary of Events and Information	Remarks and references to Appendices
1-1-16 to 8-1-16	HUPPY.	Routine work in Section. Animals evacuated by road to ABBEVILLE. Doubtful reactors to Mallein at that last among horses of Brigade returns.	
8-1-16	HUPPY.	Reaction among Bengal Horses to Mallein Test destroyed and post-mortem carried out. Reasons of Glanders were found in all their animals. Carcases burned also having been frost bitten covered with Clinical symptoms.	
9-1-16 to 31-1-16	HUPPY.	Routine work. Number of Animals evacuated by section during month - 101.	

1247 W 3299 200,000 (E) 8/14 J.B.C.&A. Forms/C. 2118/11.

SERIAL NO. 249.

Confidential

War Diary

of

Mobile Veterinary Section, Secunderabad Cavalry Brigade.

FROM 1st February 1916 TO 31st March 1916.

Army Form C. 2118.

WAR DIARY
or
INTELLIGENCE SUMMARY

Mobile Vety Section
Attention [?] Co [?]

Instructions regarding War Diaries and Intelligence Summaries are contained in F. S. Regs., Part II. and the Staff Manual respectively. Title pages will be prepared in manuscript.

(Erase heading not required.)

Hour, Date, Place	Summary of Events and Information	Remarks and references to Appendices
1-2-16 HUPPY	Routine Work.	
2-2-16		
3-2-16 ERCOURT	Changed billets - moved to ERCOURT. Billets in farm at N.W. end of village.	
5-2-16	Routine Work - Animals inoculated for A BREVILLE by Pers[?]	
19-2-16	Evacuations for month Horses 77. Mules 5.	

WAR DIARY *or* INTELLIGENCE SUMMARY

Army Form C. 2118.

2nd Indian Cavalry Brigade

Mobile Veterinary Section

(Erase heading not required.)

Hour, Date, Place	Summary of Events and Information	Remarks and references to Appendices
1-3-16 ERCOURT	Routine work. — Received orders that all cases for evacuation in Division were to be sent by road to the section and to ABBEVILLE.	
2-3-16 to 31-3-16	Routine work. — Number of animals evacuated during month. Horses 51. Mules 4.	

SERIAL NO. 249.

Confidential

War Diary

of

Mobile Veterinary Section, Secunderabad Cavalry Brigade.

FROM 1st April 1916 TO 30th April 1916.

Army Form C. 2118.

WAR DIARY
Mobile Veterinary Section (Australian) Cavalry Brigade
or INTELLIGENCE SUMMARY
(Erase heading not required.)

Instructions regarding War Diaries and Intelligence Summaries are contained in F. S. Regs., Part II. and the Staff Manual respectively. Title pages will be prepared in manuscript.

Hour, Date, Place		Summary of Events and Information	Remarks and references to Appendices
1-4-16 to 13-4-16	ERCOURT.	Routine work.	
13-4-16 to 20-4-16	ERCOURT.	Routine work.	
20-4-16 to 29-4-16	St RIQUIER.	Marched with Brigade to area ST. RIQUIER — ONEUX to Twp St Training. — Section bivies in farm outside ST RIQUIER. All horses in open and seldom sic. kept away from stables on these movements, mud to stables. Area expects will have army front horses. — keep frauds have hospital admissions are S.W. of ST RIQUIER. on flat few hospital stalled in barn in town.	
30-4-16	ERCOURT.	Billets in same place in ERCOURT as occupied prior to march. Horses in open. ROUTINE WORK. ST RIQUIER. Animals evacuated during month Horses 47. Mules 6. Total 53.	

SERIAL NO. 249.

Confidential
War Diary
of

Mobile Veterinary Section, Secunderabad Cavy. Brigade.

FROM 1st May 1916 TO 31st August 1916.

WAR DIARY or INTELLIGENCE SUMMARY

Monte Video Archives / Aide / Cavalry Brigade

Army Form C. 2118.

Hour, Date, Place	Summary of Events and Information	Remarks and references to Appendices
1-5-16 to 3-5-16 ERCOURT	Routine Work	
4-5-16		
8-5-16 ERCOURT	Division went to ST. RIQUIER area for training — this section left behind in reserve billets at ERCOURT to take on returning cases of division.	
14-5-16 ERCOURT	Division returns to manoeuvre billets.	
15-5-16 "	Veterinary cases which had been sent here for retention during training returned to their units.	
16-5-16 to 31-5-16	Routine work. Animals evacuated by road to Abbeville	

Mobile Vety Section Second eshln Cavalry Bengal

WAR DIARY
or
INTELLIGENCE SUMMARY

(Erase heading not required.)

Army Form C. 2118.

Instructions regarding War Diaries and Intelligence Summaries are contained in F. S. Regs, Part II. and the Staff Manual respectively. Title pages will be prepared in manuscript.

Hour, Date, Place	Summary of Events and Information	Remarks and references to Appendices
1-6-16 to 22-6-16 ERCOURT.	Routine work	
22-6-16 ST. RIQUIER.	Moved to Alt. RIQUIER. For training. — Ammunion renewals	
	En route to ABBEVILLE. — Bivouacked in field S.W. of town	
26-6-16 ST. RIQUIER	Moved again 7 & 8. P.M. got in to CAVILLON about 4 A.M. bivouac in field nr village	
27-6-16	Moved from CAVILLON 6 + 5 A.M. — handed to BUSSY.Le- Bivouacked in enclosed field by river	
28-6-16 to 30-6-16 BUSSY.La) DAOURS.	DAOURS: — Bivouacked in enclosed field by river Routine work — Animals exercised by train from Freshenes & Corps du Eause.	

WAR DIARY / INTELLIGENCE SUMMARY

Army Form C. 2118.

Mystic Vely. Artm. [regt?] ...Brigade

Hour, Date, Place	Summary of Events and Information	Remarks and references to Appendices
1-7-16 Burney to Damas	Moved out 3:30 A.M. with Devonshire A Section via Burney to Rikman. Stood to in arms close to Rahim Gluis. Found had to Burney at 5pm.	
2-7-16 to 12-7-16 Burney to Damas	Routine Work.	
13-7-16	Moved up to guarters at Muault – Left at 1:30 A.M.	
15-7-16 Muault {Pony, Mundabam Valley}	Moved up to guard near Burej (W. of line). Burjels moved in with fell in near Stof Work – handed over with A Battalion at 10 p.m. Marched via Burjey Farm to valley S. of Mundabam – got into valley about 3 A.M.	
14-7-16 +	Burjeds came up to Mundabam Valley about 5 A.M. – Jrn was driven to Mund Cavalrie + had to muault. Went across Wadi – got in by Cavalrie – Evacuated to K.V.S. About 150 Battle Casualties.	
16-7-16 Muault		
23-7-16	Moved back to Burey – Arrived in dhermie in Sun there.	
23-7-16 to 31-7-16 Burey	Routine Work.	

WAR DIARY
INTELLIGENCE SUMMARY

Army Form C. 2118.

Mobile Vety. Section — Australian

(Erase heading not required.)

Instructions regarding War Diaries and Intelligence Summaries are contained in F. S. Regs., Part II. and the Staff Manual respectively. Title pages will be prepared in manuscript.

Hour, Date, Place	Summary of Events and Information	Remarks and references to Appendices
1-8-16 to 7-8-16 Buissy to Daours	Routine Wk. — Horses evacuated by rail from Brackenwood to Sangles Eaux.	
8-8-16. Buissy.	Moved out at 7 A.M. today to AIRAINES — horses for night.	
9-8-16. AIRAINES	Moved out 6 A.M. today to halt hour's daily. Billed in field by river. (Borel).	
10-8-16 15-8-16 Nude hour daily.	Routine Wk.	
16-8-16.	Horses out 6 A.M. today to RIENCOURT. hour billet for night.	
17-8-16 RIENCOURT	Horses out 7 A.M. Marched to Buissy to Daours.	
18-8-16 to 28-8-16 Buissy to Daours	Breaks nor men (HALLUE) — Routine work —	
29-8-16	Horses out 9 A.M — halted to Hallein Vidame — horses for night	
30-8-16	Horses out 9 A.M. halt to NESLE NORMANDEUSE billeted in field on Bleary road.	

SERIAL NO. 249.

Confidential

War Diary

of

Mobile Veterinary Section, Secunderabad Cavalry Brigade.

FROM 1st September 1916 TO 30th September 1916

WAR DIARY or **INTELLIGENCE SUMMARY**

Army Form C. 2118.

2nd Cavalry Brigade

Hour, Date, Place	Summary of Events and Information	Remarks and references to Appendices
1.9.16 Hedle Headquarters	Took over huts at Villeroy billets in morning from Bept. F.B. Thope. In the afternoon received horses.	
2.9.16 Hedle Headquarters	Remainder of horses this morning from LONGROY GAMACHE. Radio sent in afternoon. Visits received.	
3.9.16 Hedle Headquarters	Radio sent in morning. Visited sick horses lines in afternoon. Received in afternoon two sick horses from Brigade Headquarters.	
4.9.16 Hedle Headquarters	Radio sent. Sick horses received in morning from the Bomb Horse.	
5.9.16 Hedle Headquarters	Brilliant in the evening all the horses received by the Remount train, kept there. 1 Aug. & Aug. 4/6 namely 1 Wagon Horse (12 horses), Private horses (8 horses & 2 mules), Mount Horse 18 horses, horses from Yorkshire (2 horses), Supplies (3 horse) Mr. Alley sent to Rouelle MUD on instructions of ANVD. 26/8/16 and Mr. Brighton? Received in exchange. Received orders at 7 p.m. to be ready to move at 4 a.m. following morning.	
6.9.16 Hedle Headquarters	Left Hedle had transference to gain attached to B.Echelon and marched to OISY escorting horses & mules belonging to Division Horse. 4 a.m.	

Army Form C. 2118.

WAR DIARY
or
INTELLIGENCE SUMMARY
(Erase heading not required.)

Instructions regarding War Diaries and Intelligence Summaries are contained in F. S. Regs., Part II. and the Staff Manual respectively. Title pages will be prepared in manuscript.

Hour, Date, Place	Summary of Events and Information	Remarks and references to Appendices
6/9/16 OISSY	two hours to load and was left in charge of M. DUCHAUSSY at the MAIRIE, NESTLE NORMANDEUSE, half-way between D.C. No 22 Veterinary Hospital, ABBEVILLE in regard to this horse and agricultural collection.	
7/9/16 OISSY	Left OISSY at 2 a.m. in the evening, Staff E. of AMIENS at 9.30 a.m. when watered, fed and half hour and at 10.30 returned march and arrived at BUSSY-LES-DAOURS at 12.3 p.m. Bivouacked. Received horses there taken from Canadian Cavalry Brigade.	
8/9/16 OISSY BUSSY-LES-DAOURS	Evacuated horses (43) from CORBIE. Owing to h.t. arrival of train there horses were not loaded until late in afternoon. Paid out men in evening.	
9/9/16 BUSSY-LES-DAOURS	Receiving horses in morning. Evacuated sick horses from CORBIE in afternoon.	
10/9/16 BUSSY-LES-DAOURS	Routine work. Horses for evacuation leaving the day. In the afternoon evacuated sick horses from CORBIE. Receiving sick horses during the day.	
11/9/16 BUSSY-LES-DAOURS	Routine work. Received ten sick horses and evacuated another horses from CORBIE.	

Army Form C. 2118.

WAR DIARY
or
INTELLIGENCE SUMMARY
(Erase heading not required.)

Hour, Date, Place	Summary of Events and Information	Remarks and references to Appendices
12.9.16 BUSSY-LES-DAOURS	Receiving and unsaddling horses. In the afternoon received five horses and one mule sent by of Army Remount Depot.	
13.9.16 BUSSY-LES. 10 hours	Exercising horses in the morning. In afternoon received at CAMON one horse left by 74 Field Ambulance, 24 Division. Watered in the evening on grass. One received from Pharaoh.	
14.9.16 BUSSY-LES. DAOURS	2 INDIAN Cav Divn went forward that evening. Hrs. certain remaining with "B" Echelon. Marched through DAOURS. Suffin Camp to all garments soak knives in the morning. Watered by Ambulance Mule. It was 6th 9.1 wagon and 1 Q.L. Rudor wagon gone from Ambulance Mule and two men with bushes cut down a few trees into the mud. Unchanged in evening the horses harnessed the previous day as it was abnormally drying and unfit for removal.	
15.9.16 BUSSY.LES. DAOURS.	Exercising horses in morning. At 11pm received orders to proceed to ground near ALBERT marked by Division lightly broken. Left at 10 pm, marching by way of Lavieville	

WAR DIARY or INTELLIGENCE SUMMARY

Army Form C. 2118.

Hour, Date, Place	Summary of Events and Information	Remarks and references to Appendices
16.9.16. ALBERT.	Halted at Laon and bivouacked by side of road. Had 1 Kilometre from Albert. At daybreak marched to Supply between 1st & 3rd Echelons to load. Received orders on reaching to D.C. Supply Column to return to BUSSY next day. Left at 8.30 a.m. in relation to BUSSY marching by way of QUERRIEU and arriving at 1 p.m. Very wet all interviews. On arrival found Sgt. Hardy with Mr. Young, Spence and Hargreaves from the 19 V.A. BOVEN and up for conducting party.	
17.9.16 ALBERT.		
18.9.16. BUSSY-LES-DAOURS.	Pte Weaver in charge of Mr. Kenyon, Corpl. Kennerley, Buff Taylor, Dr. Papworth, Privates Allen and Rouse reported from No.7 Veterinary Hospital for conducting party. Mrs Taylor Whipple, Snell Shaw and Ramsey reported also for orderly duty work. They came from No 8 Veterinary hospital ma 3 Cavalry division.	
19.9.16 BUSSY-LES-DAOURS	Routine work. Received air defence during the day.	
20.9.16. BUSSY-LES-DAOURS.	Evacuated in the evening from CORBIE eighteen horses in charge of Sgt. Hardy with Pte. Spence and Young.	

WAR DIARY
or
INTELLIGENCE SUMMARY

Army Form C. 2118.

(Erase heading not required.)

Hour, Date, Place	Summary of Events and Information	Remarks and references to Appendices
21.9.16 BUSSY-LES-DAOURS.	Generated from CORBIE & No 7 V.H., FORGES-LES-EAUX. Four horses and two mules. Received during the day twelve horses and one mule from the Austerlie M.V.D.	
22.9.16 BUSSY-LES-DAOURS.	Evacuated from CORBIE & No 7 V.H., fifteen horses and one mule in charge of Mr. Greenaway and Cliff. Received during the day ten wounded mules. Lieut. Copt. Reiley the Groom and Young returned in evening.	
23.9.16 BUSSY-LES-DAOURS.	Evacuated from CORBIE in the morning thirteen horses in charge of Mr Taylor & Chappell. Mr. Brown and West returned from conducting party. Received in afternoon two horses and two mules from D.D.R. & Army (Cav.) also two horses and one mule from Austerlie M.V.D. and one mule from 10 Russian Park R.E. Brown and West returned from conducting party. Serjt Pafford (from No 2 V.H. on half K.L I believe Barely Alfreton) was admitted this return by M.D.V.A.	
24.9.16 BUSSY-LES-DAOURS	Evacuated from CORBIE & No 7 V.H. six horses and four mules this morning. Received from fourteen M.V.D. twenty horses including one case of scabies range; 8 horses from Austerlie M.V.D., 3 from 7 Morgan Yards, and one from the Remount Depot.	

WAR DIARY or INTELLIGENCE SUMMARY

Army Form C. 2118.

Hour, Date, Place	Summary of Events and Information	Remarks and references to Appendices
25.9.14 BUSSY-LES-DAOURS	Concentrated from CORBIE to No. 7 U.H. Horses were lame and one sick. Received during the day thirty eight horses and two mules. In the afternoon cycled from Abbé Pont Aubergé des Rpn d'Or. Three horses rejoined AMIENS a rested man horses which had been found loose on the night of 4.9.6	
26.9.14 BUSSY-LES-DAOURS	Concentrated from CORBIE thirty five horses and two mules all attached men not on conducting parties sent to 4 Army Veterinary Clearing Station, MÉAULTE. No. 7 buffered A.V.C. and Lt. I. Nolan Barkley Depot then surrendered M.V.S. left BUSSY at 3 p.m. marching through AMIENS. Halted at BREILLY and watered horses and then pushed on to OISSY where bivouacked for night. Arrived at 9 p.m.	
27.9.14 OISSY	Routine work. In evening Sgt. Hardy and one man obtained from conducting party.	
28.9.14 OISSY	Sgt. Hardy and the six men who returned last night sent out from Railhead at HANGEST Ly of Army Veterinary Clearing Station at MÉAULTE. Ln horses received in evening from Base Horse Office work in afternoon.	
29.9.14 OISSY	Routine work.	
30.9.14 OISSY	Received orders to be ready to move. Left OISSY at 3.30 p.m. and marched to ST PIERRE à GOUAY. Bivouacked for night.	

SERIAL NO. 249.

Confidential
War Diary
of

Mobile Veterinary Section, Secunderabad Cavalry Brigade.

FROM 1st October 1916 TO 31st October 1916
                                    30th November

WAR DIARY or INTELLIGENCE SUMMARY

Army Form C. 2118.

(Erase heading not required.)

Instructions regarding War Diaries and Intelligence Summaries are contained in F.S. Regs., Part II. and the Staff Manual respectively. Title pages will be prepared in manuscript.

Hour, Date, Place	Summary of Events and Information	Remarks and references to Appendices
1 October, 1916. ST. PIERRE A GOUY	Reg. no. 13735 Pte. Rumsted / Wr. A.V.C and Lance Corporal Leigh joined outfit at reinforcements. Routine work all day.	
2 October, 1916. "	Four horses from 7 Dragoon Guards sent for treatment. Stables given possible revised and evacuated from HANGEST the same morning in charge of Pte. Brightwell. Routine work all day.	
3 October, 1916. "	Visited Third Cavalry and Fourth and fifth in afternoon. Six horses received from 7 D.G. Pte. Brightwell returned from conducting party and	
4 October, 1916. "	Reg. no. 4818 Pte. Wilton J.A.V.C. joined section at reinforcement. Three horses received from 7 Dragoon Guards. Evacuated six horses in category with Mr. Hooper.	
5 October, 1916. "		
6 October, 1916. " 7 October, 1916. "	Change. Despatched two horses from ST. SAUVEUR. Received six horses from Vet. H.2. Pte. Gossman returned. Six horses received from Rouen Horse. Horse Recovery Depot. sent to A.V.H.	
8 October, 1916. "	Received two horses from 7 Dragoon Guards and seven returning remounts. Seven horses and one mule from HANGEST in charge of Pte. Wilton and Pte. Rumsted. Routine work and Mid Hubens.	
9 October, 1916. "		

Army Form C. 2118.

WAR DIARY
or
INTELLIGENCE SUMMARY

(Erase heading not required.)

Instructions regarding War Diaries and Intelligence Summaries are contained in F. S. Regs., Part II. and the Staff Manual respectively. Title pages will be prepared in manuscript.

Hour, Date, Place	Summary of Events and Information	Remarks and references to Appendices
10 October 1916, ST PIERRE A GOUY	Routine work.	
11 October 1916, "	Mr. Gibson's Ferguson returned in evening from conducting party detailed from LE QUESNOT & horse lifting party to these horses.	
12 October 1916, "	Received two horses from the 7 Wagon Reserve and sent morning searching for horses from HANGEST. In charge of Mr Watt A.D.V.S. mobile section.	
13 October 1916, "	D.D.V.S. and A.D.V.S. mobile section.	
14 October 1916, "	Remounted for exemption worse on horse of 7 Wagon Reserve backed. One question M. Fretagne in charge and with instructions to report to O.C. No 7 Veterinary Hospital for course of instruction in use and before of clipping machine.	
15 October 1916, "	Routine work.	
16 October 1916, "	Routine work. Went to No 22 Veterinary Hospital for motor ambulance.	

WAR DIARY or INTELLIGENCE SUMMARY

Army Form C. 2118.

(Erase heading not required.)

Hour, Date, Place	Summary of Events and Information	Remarks and references to Appendices
17 October 1916 ST PIERRE A GOVT	Routine work. Received three horses from the depot. Paid men in afternoon.	
18 October 1916 "	Evacuated seven horses from HANGEST in charge of Pte. Pulkinnen. Transport inspected by D+D.S.+T	
19 October 1916 "	Routine work.	
20 October 1916 "	Routine work. Convoy three horses by rail afternoon with ambulance to No 32 Stationary hospital. Pte. Pakanen returned to unit in morning.	
21 October 1916 "	Routine work.	
22 October 1916 "	Pte. Hickmott returned in morning from No 2 Stationary Hospital. On completion of work of ambulance in need repair of spring, no brakes.	
23 October 1916 "	Routine work. Three 16 hr 32 Stationary hospital for motor ambulance.	
	Routine work. Had removal base of Bickerdike. G.A.D.V.S. Charge of motor amb. to No 32 Stationary hospital in motor ambulance.	
24 October 1916 "	Routine work	

WAR DIARY or INTELLIGENCE SUMMARY

Army Form C. 2118.

(Erase heading not required.)

Hour, Date, Place	Summary of Events and Information	Remarks and references to Appendices
25 October, 1916 ST PIERRE A GOUY	Routine work. O.O.U.A tended action and employed on sick animals.	
26 October, 1916 "	Routine work	
27 October, 1916 "	Routine work. Visited rear of units lines in afternoon.	
28 October, 1916 "	Routine work. Held a trial for 2nd of Officers' veterinary and sanitary duties.	
29 October, 1916 "	Routine work	
30 October, 1916 "	Routine work. Received one charger for 1st Bde. Also one mule from Divisional Headquarters. 1 K.O.R.L.R and one mule from 1/2 Infantry Bgde.	
31 October, 1916 "	Received from 7 Dragoon Gds, 2 horses, hacking from xx Hussars, three 3 horses. One mule and one mare from HANGEST are heavy and one mule and one mare in afternoon, for charge of Mr Gibson. Rest and now in afternoon, very heavy.	

H.W. Wyburd Capt AVC
O.C. Divisional Mobile Vet Section

WAR DIARY or INTELLIGENCE SUMMARY

Army Form C. 2118.

(Erase heading not required.)

Instructions regarding War Diaries and Intelligence Summaries are contained in F. S. Regs., Part II. and the Staff Manual respectively. Title pages will be prepared in manuscript.

Hour, Date, Place	Summary of Events and Information	Remarks and references to Appendices
ST PIERRE-A-GOUY 1 hrs. 4.9.16.	Left ST PIERRE-A-GOUY at 9 11 am and marched through by way of OISEMENT to FEUQUIERES arriving at 5.30 pm. Billeted in adjoining field.	
FEUQUIERES 2 hrs. 4.9.16.	Engaged in erecting tents mostly whare and in office routine work all day.	
FEUQUIERES 3 hrs. 4.9.16.	Routine Work. Received no dispatches from Divisional H.Q.	
FEUQUIERES 4 hrs. 4.9.16.	A.D.O.S. worked section and spent the morning looking out new huts near the railway station. Routine work all day	
" 5 hrs. 4.9.16.	Bright warm weather. Sent huts, near railway station M.L. Wham. Interviewed four candidates for party.	
" 6 hrs. 4.9.16.	G.O.C. Brigade inspected billets in the evening. Routine work.	
" 7 hrs. 4.9.16.	Received one dispatch home from Div: H.Q. Routine work during the day. Comrades Shown Service 1. No 22 M.H. by post.	
" 8 hrs. 4.9.16.	Received one dispatch home from First Squadron RE Routine work.	

WAR DIARY
or
INTELLIGENCE SUMMARY

(Erase heading not required.)

Army Form C. 2118.

Instructions regarding War Diaries and Intelligence Summaries are contained in F. S. Regs., Part II. and the Staff Manual respectively. Title pages will be prepared in manuscript.

Hour, Date, Place	Summary of Events and Information	Remarks and references to Appendices
FEUQUIERES 10 hors. g.b.	Conducted four horses to No 22 Veterinary Hospital. Received in the afternoon four horses from 11 Reserve Horse.	
FEUQUIERES 11 hors. g.b.	Conducted five Grand Hussard horses to No 22 V.H. to No 22 Veterinary Hospital. Photo Inkwist Woman. Inspected 6 Remounts (7, 14) tried no a change of bing in presence of men all been attempted. Horse is to No 22 V.H. for inoculation and care for the wound up to the wrist.	
FEUQUIERES 12 hors. g.b.	Received no horses from Field Squadron R.E. Roads work all day.	
FEUQUIERES 13 hors. g.b.	Received from Inckham Green Squadron (Remt.) 7 Wagoners Grades, 3 horses, Brigade HQ 1 horse, Dome Horse 1 horse. Evacuated 11 horses to No 22 Veterinary Hospital.	
FEUQUIERES 14 hors. g.b.	Emmanits by motor ambulance 15 to 22 Veterinary hospital, being 17 Chepper Grants and 1 horse of Inckham Green Squadron.	
FEUQUIERES 15 hors. g.b.	Visited ON.R. in morning, Received no horses from 22 V.R. nor anything sent to Reserve. Veterinary Officer.	

Army Form C. 2118.

WAR DIARY
or
INTELLIGENCE SUMMARY
(Erase heading not required.)

Instructions regarding War Diaries and Intelligence Summaries are contained in F.S. Regs., Part II. and the Staff Manual respectively. Title pages will be prepared in manuscript.

Hour, Date, Place	Summary of Events and Information	Remarks and references to Appendices
FEUQUIERES. 16th August	Received two horses from Advanced Remount Depôt Rouen. Routine work.	
FEUQUIERES 7th August	N.W.O. accompanied by 2 M.V.O. inspected about this morning Routine work. Convicts from home to No 12 Veterinary Hospital.	
FEUQUIERES 18th August	Pte. Harghaard Groome (released disabled) to No 6 Veterinary Hospital for course of instruction in carpentry of advice anything else have received from Oise Queen but 1 horses have also been Routine work all day.	
FEUQUIERES 19th August	Routine work. Men employed all day hauling about for standings.	
FEUQUIERES 20th August	Men employed drawing timber for Capt & employed in making healing procured in lieu of Dover. Horse Spt Bourns & Pte Tobbles allowed for instruction. Routine work all day Healing sheds.	
FEUQUIERES 23 August	Convicts from home to No 12 Veterinary Hospital Healing sheds.	

Army Form C. 2118.

WAR DIARY
or
INTELLIGENCE SUMMARY

(Erase heading not required.)

Hour, Date, Place	Summary of Events and Information	Remarks and references to Appendices
FEUQUIERES. 24 hrs y.d.	Routine work, men employed breaking chalk and making horse standings.	
FEUQUIERES. 25 hrs y.d.	Routine work. Ammunition lost dump from R.E. dump at Millencourt MONCOURT. Coy'd horses proceeded to England on leave in afternoon.	
FEUQUIERES. 26 hrs y.d.	Routine work.	
FEUQUIERES. 27 hrs y.d.	Escorts shown to ABBEVILLE. Men attached both on attainment.	
FEUQUIERES. 28 hrs y.d.	Routine work, breaking chalk and working on horse standings.	
FEUQUIERES. 29 hrs y.d.	Routine work & fatigues.	
FEUQUIERES. 30 hrs y.d.	Five horses and two returning cows arrived 6 ho 22 h/m ABBEVILLE in the morning, been employed making standings.	

[signature]
O.C.

SERIAL NO. 249.

Confidential

War Diary

of

Mobile Veterinary Section, Secunderabad Cavalry Brigade.

FROM 1st December 1916 TO 31st December 1916.

WAR DIARY or INTELLIGENCE SUMMARY

Army Form C. 2118.

Hour, Date, Place	Summary of Events and Information	Remarks and references to Appendices
FEUQUIERES. Hdqr.	Employed on monthly Return, and recurrent a/c's.	
2/5 Nbr.	Delivery Routine work	
6 Nbr.	Received 1 horse from 2 Dragoon Gds & 1 from Divn. Horse North invalid L/ho 22 U.H ABBEVILLE the same day	
7/8 Nbr.	Delivery Routine work	
9 Nbr.	Capt. Hawick returned from leave. Two sick had received from H Mecaw Horse.	
10 Nbr.	One sick horse received from Brigade H.Q and one stray horse from S Browne Park a.d.b. Dr. Yakurai left for England on leave.	
11 Nbr.	Routine work. One horse received from 7 Dragoons Guards.	
12 Nbr.	Received 1 horse from Browne Park and 10 from 7 Dragoon Guards. Evacuated 8 horses L/ho 22 UH ABBEVILLE	
13 Nbr.	Evacuated 2 horses L/ho 22 UH ABBEVILLE	

Army Form C. 2118.

WAR DIARY
or
INTELLIGENCE SUMMARY
(Erase heading not required.)

Instructions regarding War Diaries and Intelligence Summaries are contained in F.S. Regs., Part II. and the Staff Manual respectively. Title pages will be prepared in manuscript.

Hour, Date, Place	Summary of Events and Information	Remarks and references to Appendices
FEUQUIERES 14 Dec	Routine work as usual.	
" 15 Dec.	Received 1 horse from Rouen Horse and 1 from 7 Wagon Sheds. A.D.V.S. inspected the action	
" 16 Dec.	Received 2 horses from Rouen Horse and 1 from the xx Division Horse. Routine work.	
" 17 Dec.		
" 18 Dec.	Received one horse and one mule from the xx Division Horse. Cavalcade for horses & hr 22 UM ABBEVILLE. Returned to AVC. men in afternoon. Cavalcade one horse and one mule to hr 22 UM ABBEVILLE	
" 19 Dec.		
" 20 Dec.	Strong horse had is under command of 7 Wagon Sheds. has been received from Rouen Horse.	
" 21 Dec.	Received 1 horse from Lt. J. Hope H.Q. and one from Rouen Horse. That was evacuated to hr 22 UM ABBEVILLE the same day.	
" 22 Dec.	Routine work.	
" 23 Dec.	Routine work. Mr Pickwood returned from leave.	

WAR DIARY
or
INTELLIGENCE SUMMARY

(Erase heading not required.)

Army Form C. 2118.

Hour, Date, Place	Summary of Events and Information	Remarks and references to Appendices
FEUQUIERES 24 Dec	Routine work.	
" 25 Dec	Xmas day.	
" 26 Dec	Routine work. Mr Weyerhouse proceeded on leave to England.	
" 27 Dec	Routine work. Had post mortem on machine gun hunter with Mr Zechens Ambar. Performed post mortem for purpose of instruction.	
" 28 Dec	Routine work.	
" 29 Dec	Received 3 horses from 7 Wagon Res. Remounts we have from 7 Wagon Res. L.L. L. 22 v.m. ABBEVILLE by motor ambulance.	
" 30 Dec	Emerald Pheasant L.L. 22 V.4 ABBEVILLE. Routine work. Old wagon which is hurt was recovered from GAMACHES.	
" 31 Dec	Routine work. Closed the day instructing Private ...... who has recently in without of taking ... with outbreak of mange among his return.	

F.S. Blew Capt
26 December ...

www.ingramcontent.com/pod-product-compliance
Lightning Source LLC
Chambersburg PA
CBHW080905230426
43664CB00016B/2731